Praise for *Self Belonging*

"Unafraid to share her personal journey and vulnerabilities, Luann Robinson Hull shows us that by identifying behaviors that are hard-wired into our brains, we can then untangle them using science sprinkled with spiritual wisdom to achieve the highest expression of ourselves in relationships and in life."

> —Christy Whitman, *New York Times* bestselling author,
> *The Desire Factor*

"Through Luann's Self-Belonging personal teachings, we realize this too is our story, especially women. Her journey into and through a deeper existence of fear to love, from hurt to joy, from the biological to God Consciousness, invites authentic Self-Belonging."

> —Jean Watson, PhD, RN, FAAN, *www.watsoncaringscience.org*

"Relationships can make people crazy, even the ones who should know better. Hull's approach blends psychology, neuroscience, common self-help concepts, and a dash of spirituality—presenting it all in … results-oriented language … A polished, worthwhile self-help guide…"

> —*Kirkus Reviews*

"… highly recommended reading for self-help audiences.… Becoming a conscious game changer by examining old patterns of interaction and attraction is not an easy move, but Hull demonstrates how this can happen.… Her years of research led to breakthrough insights on brain functions and how to reprogram them by applying a mix of science and spiritual insight.

Women committed to personal growth who look for the foundations of neuropsychology tempered by new age and spiritual examination will find much to like in *Self Belonging*, which empowers readers to process their own patterns, paths, and options to embark on a better course in life."

> —*Midwest Book Review*, D. Donovan, Senior Reviewer

Self Belonging
Embrace The Wisdom Of Soul And Science
to Live Your Best Life

ALSO BY LUANN ROBINSON HULL

Happily Ever After ... Right Now:
Stop Searching for Mr. Right and Start Celebrating YOU

SELF BELONGING

Embrace The Wisdom Of Soul And Science to Live Your Best Life

LUANN ROBINSON HULL
MSW, LSCSW, D.MIN

hearn house

First Edition

ISBN: 9780983285403   (paperback)

ISBN: 9780983285410   (eBook)

Library of Congress Control Number:

Self Belonging is published by: Hearn House, LLC. PO Box 7921, Aspen, CO 81612

For information please direct emails to: Hearnhouse@gmail.com

Cover design by: Brandi Flittner, brandi.kay.riggs@gmail.com

Photo credit for images of Luann Robinson Hull: Jedidiah Gabbett, Drifting Owl Studio and Nejron

Grateful acknowledgement is made for permission to reprint the following:

"Self Portrait" from Fire in the Earth by David Whyte. Copyright © 1992 by Many Rivers Press. Used by permission of David Whyte.

"Sweet Darkness" from The House of Belonging by David Whyte. Copyright © 1997 by Many Rivers Press. Used by permission of David Whyte.

Excerpt from "East Coker" from Four Quartets by T.S. Eliot. Copyright © 1950 by T.S. Eliot, renewed 1978 by Esme Valerie Eliot. Reprinted by permission of Houghton Mifflin Harcourt Publishing Company. All rights reserved.

Excerpt(s) from How God Changes Your Brain: Breakthrough Findings From A Leading Neuroscientist by Andrew Newberg, M.D. and Mark Robert Waldman, copyright © 2009 by Andrew Newberg and Mark Robert Waldman. Used by permission of Ballantine Books, an imprint of Random House, a division of Penguin Random House LLC. All rights reserved.

"Checkmate" by Jalāl ad-Dīn Muhammad Rūmi from The Essential Rumi, translated by Coleman Barks. Copyright © 2004 by HarperOne. Used by permission of Coleman Barks.

Excerpt from The Untethered Soul by Michael Singer, copyright © 2007 by Michael Singer. Used by permission of New Harbinger Publications. All rights reserved.

"A Community of the Spirit" from Rumi: The Big Red Book by Coleman Barks. Copyright (c) 2010 by Coleman Barks. Used by permission of HarperCollins Publishers.

"Geh bis an Deiner Sehnsucht Rand/Go to the Limits of your Longing" from Rilke's Book Of Hours: Love Poems To God by Rainer Maria Rilke, translated by Anita Barrows and Joanna Macy, translation copyright © 1996 by Anita Barrows and Joanna Macy. Used by permission of Riverhead, an imprint of Penguin Publishing Group, a division of Penguin Random House LLC. All rights reserved.

Excerpt from The Road Less Traveled by M. Scott Peck, M.D. Copyright © 1978 M. Scott Peck. Reprinted with the permission of Touchstone, a division of Simon & Schuster, Inc. All rights reserved.

Every reasonable effort has been made to trace the owners of copyright materials in this book, in some instances this has proven impossible. The author and publisher will be glad to receive information leading to more complete acknowledgement in subsequent printings of the book, and in the meantime extend their apologies for any omissions.

Printed in the United States of America

Dedication

For my beloved granddaughter, Vivien.

CONTENTS

Introduction

*

There are two ways to live your life: Nothing is a miracle.
Everything is a miracle.

—Albert Einstein

From Richard's tone, I could tell he was in a simmering rage destined to escalate. "She's called the police," he said.

"She" was his former fiancé, Betty, whom Richard had left for me when we rekindled our romance from years before. Since their break-up, Richard and Betty shared custody of their dog, Prince, but rarely spoke beyond arrangements for his routine exchanges between them. Then, Prince was diagnosed with a terminal illness.

Meanwhile, my reunion with Richard had been nothing short of an emotional rollercoaster ride. Feeling we were on shaky ground and threatened by Betty's request to visit Prince at Richard's house, I put in a request to join them. That proved to be a mistake.

The ire that had been brewing within Betty since they split bubbled up suddenly in an epic eruption. During the course of that episode, she zoned in on what she likely believed would hurt Richard the most—a call to the police complaining that he was attempting to steal *her* dying dog. That cruel gesture would humiliate him, but worse, it could have robbed him of the one being with whom he truly related emotionally—Prince.

I have to ask myself why Richard caused Betty to come uncorked. After all, she's smart and beautiful, and following her split with Richard, she began dating her boss, who happens to be a celebrity. She also had a job many would envy.

INTRODUCTION

And why did Richard affect me in similar ways? How could I let him twist and torque me around like a pretzel? How had two intelligent women allowed themselves to be reduced to a cat fight over a man, when we could have been focusing our energy in far more productive ways?

While Richard certainly had some attractive attributes, he also had a violent, erratic temper. Perhaps Betty, like me, had elevated him to false idol-ship, overlooking how utterly downright mean he could be, while always hoping for the best version of him instead.

Having been advised of his possible arrest, which he blamed on me for inviting myself over, Richard commanded that I drive to his house for a proper scolding. I feared losing him if I didn't follow his directive, so I dutifully ignored my inner guidance and did as I was told.

It wasn't until my tires pierced his rocky, jagged driveway—a perfect metaphor for our relationship, that I was jarred into an important realization: I was about to approach a hurricane inside his house. So, before I lost my nerve, I mustered up the courage to turn my jeep around toward the safety of my own little tree house high in the mountains. Once there, I lay awake half the night feeling anything but safe. I was in stark terror of what might be brewing in Richard's boiler room. Where, I wondered, would I be when that fury hit full force?

It took more days of drama with Richard before my weak stance in that relationship finally collapsed under its own weight. The dog, Betty, and the police proved to be blessed catalysts that sobered me up, showed me the absurdity of my behavior, and convinced me of the drastic changes I needed to make within myself. I'd reached cliff's edge—the climax in my own story. It was then that I made the commitment to take care of myself and no one else until I'd healed from the trauma I'd experienced and allowed when connected to Richard.

Engaging in that healing process is what I've been up to for the past three and a half years, while writing this book at the same time. Over the course of that time, I was repeatedly tempted to blame Richard for being the villain who betrayed me. But what I came to realize was that as long as I projected all the blame for our toxic relationship onto him, I wouldn't be able to see my part or take responsibility for what I'd done. And, I knew that taking responsibility was the *only* way I could ever recover and change.

The process of recovery and change has required me to cultivate large doses of compassion for both myself and for Richard. Otherwise, I'd be doomed to live in torment, repeatedly scratching my head in wonder at how I could have been so embarrassingly stupid. Once the smoke cleared and I found that compassion, I could see that I'd been the one to betray myself. It's been a wonderful, difficult, gut-wrenching, amazing journey of discovery—and one that's still in progress.

Several years ago, I was honored to receive two awards for my first book about unraveling patterns that interrupt the potential for true happiness and healthy relationships. *Happily Ever After … Right Now* chronicled my own awakening from heartache and despair to transformation and joy. But it turns out that was merely a precursor to the story you now hold in your hands—a journey that (to my surprise) wasn't complete. Choosing to ignore my own warning systems, I allowed Richard back into my life. Why would a professional woman, who had spent at least a third of her existence researching and executing ways to help others avoid such traps, become ensnared in a twisted, toxic relationship—*again*?

INTRODUCTION

Revamping Our Relationships

Over the course of the past few years, I have discovered and resolved the answer to that question, among many others. And I'm delighted to report that today, I'm a happy and fulfilled single woman. Not the giddy, ecstatic type of happy, but a stable and grounded happy. Do I wake up this way every single day? No, I don't. I have my share of aches, pains, challenges, and sadness just like everyone. But I've learned to manage all of that in a completely different way than ever before—a way that really works for me, and one I believe will work for you, too.

I remain a strong advocate for relationships, intimacy, love, connection, and caring for others. It's just that I've learned over and over, that in order to be happy in an intimate relationship, you first have to be happy while you're *not* in one. When you're perfectly content without anyone else to complete you, you won't be tempted to search for someone to make you happy or expect a partner to fulfill you when you're in a relationship. That concept may seem basic. Nonetheless, I believe the syndrome of seeking Prince or Princess Charming, fraught with promises of forever bliss, has continued to influence how some of us operate, whether consciously or subconsciously.

In my view, our species must revamp the fundamental way in which we come together in partnership. As a professional who has counseled many couples with seemingly insurmountable challenges, I've rarely heard anyone take responsibility for their own despair without some serious coaching from me as their psychotherapist. Instead, just as I did at first with Richard, they'd often come to me complaining about the faults of their partner, even though that person had originally brought them bliss. Of course, when we believe it's the blessed other's job to fulfill our happiness agenda, they're bound to fail us at some point—it's just a matter of when.

Certainly, there are couples who thrive in their partnerships. Solid, intimate relationships do exist. Nonetheless, at our current level of consciousness as a species, our relationships are infused with mutual dependency or codependency, which often keeps us ping-ponging back and forth between pain and pleasure—particularly when there are issues of abuse or addiction involved.

I've seen people go through many cycles of pain and pleasure in their relationships, but I've witnessed precious few who were willing to do the work necessary to transcend those cycles. Typically, people either continue to repeat the same dance until one of them can't take it anymore. (I have participated in such a dance.) Or they somehow decide to stay together in misery rather than risk the unknown by doing the work and changing course. (I have done that, too).

My own firsthand experiences have been provocateurs, inspiring me to continue the research I started with *Happily* to study why we as a species carry such deep-seated dependency issues. For this book, I have focused on how we can learn to transcend these issues— permanently. What we want to aim for are interdependent relationships where each individual feels whole. From that place, we can decide to join with another to contribute, grow, and expand without ever losing sight of our own *core needs and desires*.

When we truly learn to overcome and rise above our maladaptive patterns, we clear our own path to flourish and develop our talents and gifts, rather than siphon off our energy and vitality into the parts of our relationships that drain us. This draining phenomenon doesn't happen because there's anything fundamentally wrong with us or our partner, but because we trigger each other's unresolved emotional pain.

How do you stop your maladaptive patterns and fully embrace yourself, so that you can go on to co-create interdependent partnerships? That's what this book will show you how to do. In writing this manuscript, I used my own life as an example of what can happen when you operate subconsciously in relationships, as well as what occurs when you become aware of how to change your own behavior. When you do, you will transcend whatever gets in the way of you and your most optimal potential—which includes having the most fulfilling relationships.

As your "personal research project," I will highlight some of my own destructive tendencies, why I believe I perpetuated those behaviors (as a woman who most certainly should have known better), and how I continue to overcome old habits (admittedly, a work still in progress). In offering my story to you, interspersed with all of the theories and teachers who have catapulted me into a completely different state of consciousness from when I started this project, my heartfelt desire is to bring you hope and healing.

Together, we'll consider how to avert the malfunctions of our minds and the resulting behaviors. We'll examine the role of our primal instincts and the conditioning that sustains them. It's essential that we maintain acute awareness of our own behaviors until we've reconditioned ourselves to "upgrade" into more favorable ways of operating— defusing the saboteurs and their influence over our powers of reasoning.

Self-Belonging

As I've mentioned, the thesis of this book is that happiness is rooted in a strong sense of personal worthiness that I have termed "self-belonging." I have learned about this personally in my own process of healing from past relationships—most recently the one with Richard. Having lived a considerable part of my life in a state of self-doubt, I've come to believe that the only way you can self-belong is to go "confidently in the direction of your dreams and live the life you have imagined." But you can only do that if you know you deserve it. You can't dream about who you are and what you have to contribute if you're preoccupied with how to fit into someone else's orbit.

On every level, you must realize that you are unique, that you matter, and that what you have to offer the world is of extraordinary value. When you do, you are destined to meet resonant souls who will support you in expanding your talents and gifts, and you theirs—all birthed in the well-spring of self-love. How do I know all of this? Because I'm living proof. I've finally moved beyond where I was once repeatedly stuck. I'm now moving in the direction of my dreams and enjoying the results of my commitment to self-belong.

The material in this book has been a labor of love that has choreographed my own process of self-belonging. Admittedly, the book is written from a personal perspective with a focus on women who find themselves in and out of unhealthy relationships. Even so, the healing models in this manuscript can be used to overcome any barriers between you and your ultimate thriving range. They transcend personality, gender, and age, and they draw wisdom from sages and scientists who have served as my treasured mentors. Ultimately, self-belonging will free you to create positive connections and relationships as you explore your strengths, gifts, passions, and life purpose.

Women: you are smart, dynamic, and beautiful, inside and out, but you may not believe me, so we have much to discuss. Men: you are much more tender and loving than you think—it's just that many of you have been influenced by the alpha male syndrome still currently alive and well in western civilization. Some of you, whether men or women, might have been making less than optimal choices in your relationships. If that's the case for you, I've mapped out some solutions in the pages ahead.

This book is a guide to connect you with your authentic self and support you in merging into your most optimal destiny, where you will discover that "everything is a miracle."

I am deeply excited for you. I truly believe with the information here, you now have the opportunity to fundamentally change your life and your relationships *forever*. I'll show you how from two lenses — first as a woman, and second as a professional psychotherapist with specialties in neuroscience, spirituality, and positive psychology.

My life's work has focused on human consciousness and behavior. Over the course of my twenty-five-year career, as well as my personal history, I've been inspired to explore why we humans engage, react, and respond the way we do, particularly when many of our habits and propensities cause us so much misery and pain. I'm repeatedly fascinated by my findings, which I offer to you here in *Self Belonging*.

The Game Plan

The following are some highlights from the chapters ahead:

Chapter One: *Self-Belonging—A Conversation*

This chapter considers the current state of humanity, some of our human frailties, and how we can outgrow our problems and focus more on what the late psychiatrist Carl Jung termed, "the life urge."

Chapter Two: *The Human Upgrade*

Here, I explore how paying attention and engaging in the art of awareness can help us eliminate the cyclical dramas we often experience in our relationships. We can achieve a human upgrade, which expands our potential for happiness.

Chapter Three: *How Conditioning Influences Relationships*

I examine what goes wrong when you're driven by

subconscious conditioning and how to take steps to change.

Chapter Four: *How Happiness Gets Hijacked*

I evaluate the process of conditioning in more depth and look into why certain behavioral patterns form and persist. The work of cellular biologist, Bruce Lipton and neuroscientist, Joseph LeDoux, will serve as our guide. Lipton's research has indicated that our cells and genetic expressions can be altered by positive or negative thoughts, and LeDoux's findings show how our biological drives influence human emotion.

Chapter Five: *Conscious Evolution: Becoming a Game Changer*

This chapter shows how the history of your biology continues to influence your current behaviors, drives, and attachments. I also demonstrate the importance of waking up to your patterns—particularly the ones that have kept you sequestered and stuck.

Chapter Six: *Becoming the Master of Your Awareness*

In this segment, I talk about Barbara Hand Clow's book, *Awakening the Planetary Mind,* in which she examines the overarching psychological patterns in the collective consciousness and subconscious. Awareness of these patterns will help you become more radically compassionate—both with yourself and others—as you explore the nature of fear, the science of epigenetics, and your own hero's/heroine's journey.

Chapter Seven: *Sweet Darkness*

In this chapter, we deep-dive into the subject of

dependency, attachment, and addiction. You'll learn how to amp up your self-regulation circuits in order to avoid these common traps.

Chapter Eight: *Sweet Freedom*

Here, we explore the effects of patriarchal authority, group think, Rupert Sheldrake's theory of morphic resonance, the possible influence of karma, and the powerful prescriptive practice of Ho'oponopono. These topics lead us to what scientists and sages say—that conscious, compassionate awareness is the key to enlightenment.

Chapter Nine: *Black Widow and Captain America Share the Airspace*

In my adventure of learning to thrive alone, I share how I've finally found the love of my life—myself. A work in progress, which I suspect I will be for as long as I draw breath, I'm finally happy in my own skin with my own life. If someone else who is a match shows up to join me as I complete this journey, I'll be happy. If he doesn't, I'll be happy. *So will you.*

Epilogue: *Self-Belonging—The Inner Place of Grace*

In this final part of the book, I revisit Jung's quote on "outgrowing insoluble problems" as a way to support you in measuring your progress. Are you stepping into your Divine blueprint, which will accelerate your evolutionary plan and support your optimal potential? You'll explore how love can be the magic catalyzer that can expand your consciousness and affect the minute workings of your DNA.

SELF BELONGING

*Go confidently in the direction of your dreams and live
the life you have imagined.*

—*Henry David Thoreau*

ONE

Self Belonging — a Conversation
*

Sit in the seat of your Self Belonging
Wake down into the depths of your soul
Rise up and meet your heart's longing
To have a conversation with the world
Let love be your midwife
As you birth into form
All that aches to be born
From the Spirit that lives in you

—LRH, Christmas Eve, 2011

It was an extraordinary gentleman named Naj who first introduced me to the phrase "self-belonging." At the tender age of seven, he faced his most profound fear—being abandoned by his parents. He was sent to a boarding school in England far away from his homeland of Iran with no advance preparation from his family about what was going to happen to him. They simply deposited him there and left without warning. For two years, he wasn't allowed any contact with his mother, father, or siblings.

A few days after his parents left him at the school, Naj came to believe they were never coming back. Night after night, he cried himself to sleep. Just about the time he'd given up all hope of ever feeling loved again, he decided to let himself dive into the depth of

19

his desolation and despair. "It was oddly comforting to do so," he told me. "As I allowed the misery to completely wash over me, I had a very interesting epiphany: since there doesn't seem to be anyone else to belong to in my new world, I will belong to myself."

The experience led this young boy to deep inner peace, which he has since termed self-belonging. "Somehow, as young as I was, I sensed that I was deeply connected to an internal influence that was stronger than my fears of abandonment, however daunting those had become. I knew I was not alone—that there was a force greater than my little, local self, literally energizing me to survive this experience—in fact actually helping me to embrace it. That influence has never abandoned me. Even during the overthrow of the Shah of Iran in the 1970s, when I had to evacuate my family from our homeland, it guided me through all danger."

Despite the fact that Naj had been completely separated from his parents or any nurturing adult during a critical time of his development, he managed to access feelings of self-love, which he believes emerged from his connection to what he describes as "the Indwelling God." His access point to this inner guidance system became available only when he was able to face and surrender to his fear about what would become of him in this strange land away from everyone he loved.

Today, Naj is a committed husband, supportive father, cherished friend, devoted spiritual servant, generous philanthropist, and successful businessman. And he continues to attribute every triumph and achievement in his life to the foundation of self-belonging, which he has cultivated ever since that pivotal evening which served as his launch pad to self-awareness. How can the rest of us cultivate a similar state of being, and what prevents us from doing so naturally and automatically?

A New Level of Consciousness

Renowned psychiatrist Carl Gustav Jung explained that we become limited by fear-based conditioning in childhood and by patterns/habits that result from this conditioning. He believed, however, that we can transcend the influence of our fear-based habits by "broadening our outlook" and moving into a "new level of consciousness":

> *All the greatest and most important problems of life are fundamentally insoluble.... They can never be solved, but only outgrown. This "outgrowing" proved on further investigation to require a new level of consciousness. Some higher or wider interest appeared on the patient's horizon, and through this broadening of his or her outlook the insoluble problem lost its urgency. It was not solved logically in its own terms but faded when confronted with a new and stronger life urge.*

About a year before my conversation with Naj, my own patterns resurfaced with Richard, the man I'd left several years earlier. I had researched, written, and lived the material from my first book, *Happily Ever After ... Right Now,* and believed I was immune from losing balance in my relationships. I'd been living a peaceful life on a mountaintop in the Rockies and was liberated (I thought) from the dysfunctional patterns that inspired many of the insights in *Happily,* while moving deeper into a joyful relationship with myself.

But it turned out that despite all my study and research on the subject of human consciousness, I still carried internal obstacles that needed to "lose their urgency." After listening to Naj about self-belonging, I knew I had to confront the raw and rugged emotional quagmire in which I'd immersed myself—yet another time.

Our conversation was the well-timed memo that catapulted me out of the drama with Richard. Facing my fears, like Naj had done, helped me realize that I could, powerfully and intently, belong to myself and allow love to be my "midwife." But fortitude is required to sit in that "seat of belonging," and I have certainly tested my level of endurance.

Even though I'd written an entire book on the myth of Prince Charming before my relationship with Richard, I clearly carried enough internal bait to catch and feed that myth one more time. When I let myself get hooked again, it wasn't really by Richard himself, but by my ideal of what I thought he was capable of resolving for me. I had continued to be mistaken about what would satisfy my internal longing. Simply put, even though my head knew better, my heart wasn't quite ready to release the fairytale.

I don't blame myself for believing once more in magic. After all, the Prince Charming myth is both insidious and pervasive on planet Earth. And I'm not, nor will I ever be, immune from its influence. It is, after all an insoluble problem. Therefore, I have to continue to be hypervigilant and aware of it.

In my view this particular myth is one of the *most* insoluble problems of our human condition—that something or someone could somehow save us from the inevitable misery and longing we all experience.

Of course, everyone wants relief, so the natural inclination is to go looking for an answer. But our longing *cannot* be resolved by an external solution—whether it be a lover, spiritual guru, or winning the lottery. As it turns out, this glorious longing is undoubtedly the most Divine of all gifts (however well disguised it may appear). Its purpose is to notify us that there is a mighty "life urge," as Jung put it, that dwells at the core of our being. Answering the call to that life urge can only be accessed through the broadening of our outlook—this we do by turning within for resolution. In doing so, the problem of our attachments to anything or anyone in our external orbit will fall away, and the life urge will well up from inside with a volcano of passion and creativity, which is the *true* source of happiness and well-being.

How do I know this? Because as I said, I'm your personal research project, having experienced firsthand the effects of that life urge welling up and building in momentum from the inside.

The evening I met Naj, I realized that if a little boy at the age of seven, who had been virtually abandoned by his parents ("for his own good," they would later tell him), could access his life urge, it was possible for me to do the same. Naj's ability to outgrow his own insoluble problem on that lonely night in a cold, English dormitory provided me with a remarkable example of how facing our fears will create a breakthrough—every single time. His story propelled me into a journey of discovery on how to truly self-belong, to outgrow my own insoluble problems, and then share my findings with you.

So, I encourage you to stop searching for an outside solution to resolve the insatiable longing that tugs at your soul. When you pause that search and take a breath, you'll clearly see that this longing is sustained, nurtured, and fed by a belief that something "out there" is more powerful than what is within you. When you finally begin to claim your own power, you realize that the *source of rescue from your suffering will always be found in the stillness of your very own being—at the root of your self-belonging.* This is so even when the entanglements in your mind want you to believe otherwise—that you need someone or something to save you.

Unraveling the entanglements of the mind and the tricks it can play on us can be particularly challenging in romantic relationships. After all, where and when do we feel the most vulnerable and afraid? The answer for me has always been in my most intimate connections, where the stakes seem to skyrocket into epic proportions. And, of course, what I have repeatedly learned the hard way is that the biggest sacrifice to my soul happens when I abandon my own precious back. I do this by not being true to my sense of self-respect, self-love, and personal dignity.

Based on my own experiences and the stories I've heard, we must somehow get beyond patterns of behavior that can perpetuate our insoluble problems. We have to be willing to uncover, neutralize, and move past whatever may impede the expansion of our outlook. Doing so is what paves the way for that "new level of consciousness."

Cultivating the art of self-belonging is about nurturing this process. In continuing to overcome limiting beliefs and behaviors, we create an opening to the place where seemingly insoluble problems will lose their urgency. And, in order to do so, we must challenge the old familiar patterns, habits, and ways of coping. We have to recruit courage, faith, and a sense of personal power, which are all an integral part of the self-belonging package.

Outgrowing Our Human Frailty

As a species, we humans are fundamentally primates, so our minds are a morass of entanglements that keep us endlessly tempted by distractions and triggers that create havoc and misery. We lose keys, forget names, and misinterpret situations by making false assumptions based on our personal experience, emotional sensitivity, and fundamental model of the world.

We default to programs within us of deeply buried survival strategies created from past traumas. These patterns and habituated ways of coping that Jung talked about are a subconscious effort to bypass future pain. What I've come to realize over time, however, is that these strategies, which are designed to avoid suffering, are actually anchored in sand. Therefore, when something triggers us, our psyche instantly relives a prior trauma or disturbance. Something in the present rekindles a subconscious memory, causing us to react with fear or anxiety, which can easily overrule reason.

For most of us, triggers for these episodes are everywhere, from bee stings to stinging words, to the harsh behavior of others. According to Bruce Lipton, cellular biologist and internationally recognized leader in bridging science and spirituality, these triggers can cause us to spin off new beliefs or reinforce preexisting patterns of coping (old beliefs) that are already stored in our subconscious databanks where ninety-five percent of our behavior originates.

Christiane Northrup, a board-certified physician and leading authority in women's health and wellness states, "Your beliefs and thoughts are wired into your biology. They become your cells, tissues, and organs. There is no supplement, no diet, no medicine, and no exercise regimen that can compare with the power of your thoughts and beliefs."

These subterranean belief systems can cause knee-jerk reactions to experiences occurring in present time. Lipton says, "In order to secure our future, we must empower ourselves with the knowledge of who we are. With an understanding of how our programming shapes our lives and the knowledge of how we can change that programming, we can rewrite our destiny."

With that knowledge and understanding, we can face our inner disturbances as they arise, while allowing them to move through, up, and out of us. We have to learn to resist being persuaded by the conditioned reactions that trap these disturbances in our psyche.

As we journey together in cultivating the art of self-belonging, you'll learn how to do just that—change your programming and rewrite your destiny.

Conscious "God" Awareness—Conscious Evolution

Some spiritual traditions hold that spontaneous flashes of insight like Naj had on the night of his self-belonging epiphany are shifts of consciousness, which can lead to enlightenment. In this state, insoluble problems are released, shifting our attention toward the greater life urge, or Naj's idea of the Indwelling God. Jung's quote provides us with a framework to keep track of our progress by noticing whether or not we are outgrowing the hold that insoluble problems have on us. Are these problems losing their urgency? Are we keeping our focus steadied on the life urge that stimulates spiritual breakthroughs and inspires creativity and insight?

Famed humanistic psychologist Abraham Maslow referred to the state of enlightenment as "self-actualization" or "self-realization." In his famous hierarchy of human needs theory, it's the most expanded state or the final level of psychological development attainable when all basic needs, such as physiological, safety, love, and esteem, are met.

What does Maslow mean, and what is Carl Jung saying when he talks about a new level of consciousness? Just what is enlightenment, self-actualization, self-realization, or conscious awareness? In *The Road Less Traveled*, the late Scott Peck offered a simple explanation for the word "conscious." He said it's derived from the Latin prefix *con*, meaning "with" and the word *scire*, meaning "to know." So "becoming conscious is *to know with our consciousness*," which, Peck points out, ultimately means to know God. Therefore, he believed, the development/expansion/evolution of consciousness has to do with bringing information stored in our subconscious mind into our conscious mind. It's a process of our conscious "God mind" coming into synchrony with the subconscious mind.

How can we train ourselves to know whether we're reacting to life by letting a habit guide our actions or words, or responding from a place of conscious God awareness? Peck says that as you practice communion with your developing consciousness (of knowing God), there will be "enough joy to sustain you" through all of your moments of discomfort. Therefore, you will be less and less likely to become snared by triggers or distractions. Also, even though you will still have times of intense loneliness, which inevitably accompany a spiritual journey, you won't ever feel completely alone because you'll know in every fiber of your being that the Internal Divine is your constant companion. This realization, however miraculous it might seem for an abandoned little boy to experience, is likely what came to Naj when he had his spiritual breakthrough at the moment of his deepest despair.

So what exactly is the nature of this information being held in the subconscious mind? Bruce Lipton says that the subconscious part of our mind is the registry of data that we've collected over our lifetime. It often runs our behaviors when we aren't aware. This under-the-radar/behind-the-scenes storage tank contains massive amounts of information, yet its downloads are hardly selective. Though while at times it can eclipse the conscious mind—it is in no way smarter. Therefore, it's up to us to become aware of our thoughts, behaviors, and patterns so that we can take steps to merge our conscious and subconscious minds. The more alert we are to our propensities and reactions, the more we can build a foundation for self-realization/self-actualization/self-belonging/ultimate God consciousness.

In other words, move from actor to director in the story of your life, or freely switch roles once you have full command of the dialogue. But don't sit back and allow a gathering of extras to call for the action or make the cuts.

Responding or Reacting to Life: Practicing Awareness

We can begin to mitigate the effects of our knee-jerk reactions when we make a commitment to unwind our busy mind, strengthening the areas of our brain that can negotiate more reasonable responses to our triggers.

According to surgeon and chronic pain specialist David Hanscom, "Practicing awareness is the first step in reprogramming your brain — the easiest technique to explain, and the most difficult to consistently use." Even so, there are simple, scientifically proven practices that can help undo the habits and conditioning that repeatedly overrule your conscious awareness. As the material in *Self Belonging* unfolds, you'll learn about the science of neuroplasticity — or how the brain can literally change itself through techniques that negotiate and balance the pressures of both physical and emotional pain.

You're meant to thrive across all areas of your life — emotionally, spiritually, physically, and mentally. As you cultivate your own sense of self-belonging like Naj began to do as a small boy, you'll discover that despite whatever is happening in your external world, you can *always* choose to flourish from the inside out. When others in your orbit make choices that aren't in alignment with your values, ideology, or truth, you won't be tempted to try and "fix" them. When you realize what's going on doesn't work for you, and you see no evidence of change through your attempts to negotiate, you have one of two choices: accept the person or situation exactly as is or fully let go and move on.

While contemplating your choices, you can ask yourself some important questions. "Am I making good use of the great gift of life? Am I responding or reacting to life? Am I compromising myself or my life path in any way?" In contemplating your answers, consider

28

how you want to spend the rest of your precious life—and with whom.

You are meant to thrive across all areas of your life—emotionally, spiritually, physically, and mentally.

The Art of Connecting

Brené Brown, research professor at the University of Houston's Graduate College of Social Work, has spent the majority of her career studying human relationships through the lens of vulnerability, courage, and authenticity, and how these qualities relate to our sense of love and self-worth. I, too, am a social worker. For the past twenty-five years, I've engaged in my own research project—the study of human consciousness with a focus on relationships—how we connect to ourselves and to one another. Admittedly, I've embarked on this research in part to chip away at my own issues with the lofty goal of helping humanity at the same time. Some of my findings are documented in *Happily Ever After ... Right Now,* which supports readers in avoiding the search for external solutions to happiness, while looking within to discover their life purpose and passions.

Brown says, "We are neuro-biologically wired to desire a sense of belonging—to be connected." In her research over the course of a ten-year longitudinal study, she found that the most significant barrier to connecting with another person is *the feeling of unworthiness* (the absence of self-belonging), which may trigger an impulse to shut down. She noted that if we "numb-out" our willingness to be vulnerable, we become less likely to feel other sensations, such as joy, rapture, peace, and of course, love—virtually anesthetizing our most beautiful human feelings. Therefore, in order to truly connect with another, we have to be willing to "see into ourselves the all of who we are," and then let others see us in the same way. To do so is to live life authentically and wholeheartedly.

How can we allow the gift of transparency—of letting ourselves be "fully seen"? Are you (am I?) willing to chip away at the layers of concrete that you've carefully poured around your heart so that no one will know the truth of who you *really* are? What are you hiding in that heart-chamber anyway? Isn't it possible that there might be some buried treasure in there?

If you *really* look, you'll see that, despite a few stains and imperfections, you want to live life with your whole heart. If you didn't, you wouldn't be reading the words on this page. So, if you're willing, please join me as you continue reading, in excavating some of your own buried treasure—even if it may be intermingled with stuff you don't want to see.

The substance, stories, and wisdom we'll tap into in the following pages will support you in digging into the dark corners of your soul, while systematically helping you unearth and discard anything that may interrupt you from reaching your optimal potential, a new level of consciousness, and conscious God awareness.

But be forewarned: if it doesn't feel a bit strange, awkward, and unfamiliar, you're probably not going deep enough. Get ready to sharpen your chisel, and be prepared to carve your way into unprecedented territory. This is where your true gifts and talents for creativity, healthy connections, and thriving across all areas of your life await your loving attention.

If you take the risk to proceed in this direction, you'll be rewarded by becoming more proficient at transcending all that has complicated your life. You will then be guided to attain more expanded states of inner peace, self-love, and self-belonging. I believe it's possible to pave the way for a sweeping shift in the consciousness of humanity. As you and I commit to breaking through old, lifelong patterns and habits that have held us captive, God consciousness will repeatedly emerge as the guiding influence in our lives, supporting us in participating in that shift.

This God-Consciousness influence is certain to usher in a new standard for the life every single one of us deserves to live. As part of a more cooperative, interconnected, and compassionate way of being, we're participating in a global epidemic, which has the potential to cause the insoluble problem of unhealthy dependency in relationships to lose its urgency. Maybe it can eventually fall away for good.

TWO

The Human Upgrade

*

*The first desire is the longing for purpose, the drive to become
who you are meant to be.
This desire is the longing to fulfill your potential and contribute to
the world.*

—*Rod Stryker*

In *The Four Desires*, author and Yoga master Rod Stryker offers his
theory that each of us has a fundamental longing to fulfill our purpose,
optimize our potential, and make our contributions. He suggests that
when your "deepest driving desire" is in alignment with this purpose,
you will thrive, exponentially enhancing your happiness potential.

Several years ago, on February 13th, fulfilling my life purpose
was the last thing on my mind. Perhaps, as I was lying face down
on an operating table, some awareness of Stryker's wisdom could
have saved me some significant suffering. Instead, I was focused on
Richard. *Where was he?*

The patient nurse holding my hand, instructed, "Don't move,"
while another attendant slathered slippery gunk on my spine.

What if I twitch or something? I pondered, while longing for Richard.
I wanted out of there.

I should send the nurse to the waiting room, I thought. *Richard
might be there. Wait—I hear someone coming. Maybe Richard?*

No. It was the doctor who was going to inject steroids into my

32

spine. This was an attempt to relieve the pain from a chronic migraine headache I'd had since before Christmas. "There will be a brief sting," the doctor warned.

That's what they always say, I thought. *Breathe. That's it. One more breath. Sweet Jesus, this hurts.*

But the truth of the matter was this: a much deeper pain had been brewing amidst the craziness in which I'd been a willing participant with Richard. Therefore, I had to come to terms with the fact that my image of him in the waiting room was nothing more than a fantasy. He had forgotten to come — to be there for me when I really needed him, and his absence was to be expected.

That's how it was with Richard. He would frequently fail to call or show up. Even so, I kept believing he was going to drop the Mr. Hyde part of his Jekyll and Hyde dual personality. For it seemed whenever he fell short or flew into a rage, he'd come swooping back in, tempting me with roses, prose, and promises, while dripping in charm. But inevitably, his romantic self would flicker and fizzle out like a firefly losing its life force, and he'd switch back into the dark, distant, detached, man who always reemerged when he felt I was all in again.

The day after he failed to show up for my medical procedure was, of course, Valentine's Day, so, predictably, he appeared at my door toting a card and flowers, accompanied by all the familiar tools of seduction that had repeatedly won me over. Once again, I opened the door and continued going around in romantic circles with him. I became more anesthetized with every passing day that I stayed. Yet, just like my surgeon's efforts in vain to numb the sting of his needle, I couldn't stop the ongoing pain in this relationship with a two-faced man.

One was a face, often brutal, that was revealed to me behind closed doors. The other was his public face — the spiritual, professional, pillar-of-the-community type of guy. I desperately wanted to believe that the latter was the real face—a man of kindness, commitment, and integrity.

I'm hardly alone in this brand of illusion.

Thirty-four-year-old Jennifer watched in horror as her husband, Matthew, killed their infant daughter in a fit of rage. In the words of the prosecutor, "the tiny, two-month-old died when Matthew spiked her like a football." Matthew was well-known to Child Protective Services following a series of abuse reports. After completing mandatory anger management classes, he was able to convince Jennifer that he had changed, persuaded her to allow him back into their home, and soon exploded into the fury that resulted in their child's brutal death.

I wonder how much Jennifer believed in the fantasy of a happy future instead of the horrors of her history with the man who eventually murdered their child.

Then, there's Lance Armstrong's girlfriend, Anna Hansen. According to the *Aspen Times*, (a photograph showed Armstrong's vehicle missing a left headlight and scrunched like an accordion on the driver's side):

> *The Aspen Police Department provided the media photographs of a sports utility vehicle belonging to world-famous cyclist Lance Armstrong. Armstrong, who owns a home in Aspen's West End, was driving the vehicle December 28 when he hit two parked cars following a party, police said. His girlfriend, Anna Hansen, initially told police that she was the driver who hit the vehicles…*

How could Anna justify putting herself at risk for arrest in order to protect her infamous boyfriend? How could any of us go back to these men over and over, despite the evidence that they were not going to change?

Sharing these scenarios is *not* for the purpose of telling sad stories—mine or anyone else's—or for inflicting self-blame, blaming other women for staying in relationships fraught with abuse, neglect, or both, or for even blaming the men profiled in the aforementioned scenarios. Instead, I want to point out the critical need for becoming aware of any obstacles that get in the way of our emotional health and well-being.

From what I have learned both professionally and personally on my journey into conscious awareness, there's no room for victims, villains, or rescuers. In *Happily*, I state, "victims are volunteers." Regardless of the roles we play or the stories we tell, we are each ultimately responsible for our own lives. So, if something isn't working out for us, we *can* be the change that will catapult us beyond our challenges. Once again, I'm living proof.

A few months after the ordeal in the hospital, I finally chose myself and have never looked back. My migraine headache lifted within four days of my decision to leave Richard—even after steroid injections and other interventions had failed to bring relief. I'd outgrown the pain, supported by the magic elixir of self-love and the life urge, which became the subject of my higher and wider interest. It was then that I set course for a life of self-belonging—the path that I'll share with you as you continue reading.

Being Aware—Paying Attention

Prior to the unraveling of my relationship with Richard, I had spent the previous twenty-five years of my professional life studying the aberrations and difficulties in human relationships. As a clinical therapist, I supported a multitude of others in successfully resolving their challenges. Why, then, couldn't I immediately fix things in my own life? Despite all of my years of training and culling my experience in a book devoted to the subject of self-love, it has taken me a long time to master the art of belonging to myself. Even now, after all my study and research, my insights can still be hi-jacked by my emotions, patterns, and subconscious tendencies. Being aware and paying attention is truly an art form and I am a work in progress.

Based on both my personal and professional experience, I believe we are all products of our conditioning and ancestry. We're naturally attracted to and repeatedly move toward circumstances that are familiar. This propensity causes us to develop habits that make us feel safe. Unfortunately, following the familiar, habituated path doesn't always ensure our safety, health, or well-being.

For example, in contemplating Anastasia Steele's behavior, the main fictional character in *Fifty Shades of Grey,* as much as I hate to admit it, I can see similarities between Ana and me. The book is about a twisted, toxic relationship that focuses on a man (Grey) tormented by internal demons and obsessed with control. He becomes fixated on Ana, who allows him to mistreat her and take advantage of her due to her unhealthy attraction to him.

Why were more than 100 million people so fascinated with the dark subject matter of this book and film? Like me, I believe that many people (particularly women) could identify with Ana and how she lost herself in that unhealthy relationship.

Tom Graff, a wise colleague and clinical psychologist practicing in Wichita, Kansas, put into perspective what can happen when our conditioning spills into intimate relationships:

> *If your past conditioning is directing things, which can often be the case when we are not aware, it is possible that you will replicate the behavior of one parent (however favorable or unfavorable that*

*behavior is) and marry or partner with one who is a
lot like the other (regardless of how s/he conducted
her/his life).*

Fortunately, by *paying attention* and engaging in the art
of *awareness,* I was finally able to eliminate my cyclical drama with
Richard by being alert to how my conditioning was spilling into that
relationship. Even so, I'm not going to pretend that this work isn't
challenging. When brought to my knees by what had kept me stuck, I
finally began to feel how badly I was hurting. At that point, something
unexpected happened. My faith began to kick in. I came to the
realization that there was nothing else left to do other than to believe
more in God than I did in my little, local self and what she thought
was best for me. Slowly, steadily, I began to realize that the Divine
wanted so much more for me than I was willing to allow myself to
have by staying in an emotionally abusive relationship.

Those flashes of insight were quite brief in the beginning—
only tiny blips across the radar screen of my conscious awareness.
My anxious fears and imagination had been deeply conditioned.
Therefore, I needed to repeatedly remind myself of two things: 1) I
had been brought to my knees, and 2) the only rescue would be Divine
intervention. Period.

Admittedly, in the beginning, I had only a mustard seed of that
faith. At times, it would leave me entirely. Nonetheless, I knew I
didn't want to drop to the floor again. So, I did whatever I had to do to
keep myself upright—repeatedly praying like hell for the strength and
courage to stand tall, while having nightly gratitude for another day of
being able to put one foot in front of the other.

Making a commitment to self-belong can feel challenging at first.
Even so, it doesn't have to be that hard if you stop in your tracks right
now and realize the rewards that await you when you make a decision

to be on your own side. In doing so, you will choose *only* to be in conscious, loving relationships, while letting go of ones that aren't. You'll continue recruiting the indomitable will to let go of anything and anyone that doesn't support you before you're overpowered, as I was. Once you pivot in the direction of self-love, you'll always be cared for ("earth angels" will show up everywhere), you *will* survive, and eventually,\, you *will* thrive. How do I know? I'm your personal research project, and I have not only survived, but I am, indeed, thriving. I'll address the practices and science that have supported me as we go forward in our self-belonging journey together.

As you continue to make progress, you'll feel deep compassion for yourself and whatever you endured in living through some of the ordeals of your past. Ultimately, you will also feel compassion for others, particularly for those you feel have caused you the most pain. You'll understand that it was their own subconscious patterns that emerged when the two of you decided to dance together.

When you're able to overrule your emotional responses with reasoning, discernment, and Divine support, you'll be on the precipice of expanding into an upgrade in your inner operating system. In seeing that a situation is insoluble, you will take the lesson of that situation and let go. Once you do, you'll be free to turn your attention to the life urge coursing through your body and soul. When you focus on that life urge, the insoluble problems will lose their urgency and eventually dissolve for good.

In the meantime, it helps to remember that every person, place, and circumstance brings us bouquets of blessings, however well-disguised they might appear at any given time. In my case, had it not been for Richard, I may never have been able to see a destructive pattern of behavior that I'd perpetuated for decades—in spite of my training and knowledge on the subject of human relationships. From where I stand now, I see the value in my time with him. That said, please note that it isn't necessary to take the path of learning that I unwittingly chose. With education and awareness, you *can* change without having to endure such painful ordeals.

As we continue, I will show you how to be aware when your behavior is likely driven by a subconscious motivator. Together, we can consider new approaches that will support you in seeing and transcending these unhealthy tendencies.

You will learn how to give your heart something else to do so that you're no longer tempted to go off on an emotional binge with the person who is hurting you. And you'll learn how it feels to simply live your life from a foundation of peace and contentment—regardless of whatever bombs might seem to be going off in your external world. You'll discover how to sidestep the explosives or avoid being around them altogether.

And through this process, you'll discover a treasure chest of passion and power poised to catapult your creative nature into action—guaranteed. Once you begin to see how the tricks of your subconscious conditioning repeatedly play out—when you start catching them in action—you will connect more often and more deeply to the inner wisdom that has been guiding you to find your way all along. I believe the sparks fueled by your own internal guidance will eventually combust into a bonfire of love, creativity, and passion, where you were always meant to dwell.

Without having to analyze or judge every disturbance on your path, you'll gradually see and feel just how life wants to express itself through the unique lens that is you. Living with that level of awareness will activate unprecedented states of joy and freedom. How do I know? Because, as previously mentioned, I am your personal research project. And while taking on that role has been difficult at times, I'm fortified by the benefits. Despite my near maddening regressions, I can see the light— flickering and dim on occasion, but brilliant at its source, illuminating the freedom and happiness that is my birthright.

The Human Upgrade

My curiosity about the human condition has played out in both professional and personal arenas. It has taken me everywhere from an ashram in India to a Doctoral Ministry program, where I studied human consciousness through the lens of philosophy and spirituality. I have also participated in countless workshops and immersions, either as a participant or facilitator. When I left my life as a psychiatric social worker in the 1990s, I was seeking information outside what seemed to be a myopic view of the causes and cures for aberrant behavior. What really is the root reason for people's heads going haywire? Why do some who are exposed to extreme trauma have Post-Traumatic Stress Disorder, while others with the same level of contact with that trauma seem mostly unaffected? What are the trip-wires in the brain that cause mood and personality disorders? Can the pathways inside our skulls be rewired, bypassed, or transcended altogether in ways that effect positive change without exposure to the unpredictable consequences of psychotropic drugs? Why does one son of a narcissistic, sociopathic father follow that lineage of behavior while another turns out to be a gentle, kind man, loving husband, and father? Why are some more inclined to fall prey to their desire for dopamine highs? (Dopamine neurons are released in the brain when something pleasurable occurs, inducing a state of gratification. We will continue discussing the effects of this neurotransmitter in subsequent chapters.) These highs can be delivered in many forms — from drugs, to relationships, gambling, shopping, food, etc. Cravings for these highs can lead to dependency, diminished self-regulation, and ultimate addiction.

I literally saw hundreds of patients go through the hospital, and I've participated in countless staff meetings arranged to determine how they could be supported in getting neutral enough to return to their lives—lives of struggle and often desperation.

But what about going *beyond* neutral into the happiness zone? Back then, doctors were vigilant about containing patient stays in order to appease the managed care watch dogs who threatened to shut us down if we retained people beyond the measures permitted by third party payers (i.e. insurance companies). Now some twenty-five years later, with the U.S. saddled by a fractured health care system, I suspect the situation is even worse.

Ever since I walked away from that world, I have been researching those questions. In the chapters that follow, we will continue to unravel and make some sense of my findings on the mysteries of human consciousness and the relationships that emerge from that consciousness. I am convinced that it's possible for our species to move from its manic-depressive adolescent phase into a mature, conscious adulthood.

In Chapter Three we'll look at how our conditioning influences our relationships, what can go wrong when we're driven by this subconscious conditioning, and how to be aware of what we're doing so that we can take steps to change.

THREE

How Conditioning
Influences Relationships

*

*In the depths of our being, in body, mind, and spirit, we know
intuitively that we are created to love and be loved, and that
fulfilling this imperative, responding to this vocation, is the
central meaning of our life.*

—Sam Keen

Unraveling this conundrum of loving and being loved is a riddle
worth resolving. It seems to be wrapped up in a labyrinth of emotions,
conditioning, patterns, gene pools, karma (the consequences of
actions by us and others), and the influences of our environment.
How can we live well in these magical body-suits, replete with their
pre-existing conditions? Is it possible to expand beyond the chaos
that seems to scramble all of our insights about who we really are?
How can we keep our focus steadied on Carl Jung's notion of the
life urge?

I suspect that most of us are driven by subconscious reservoirs
of stuff that repeatedly diminish the force of that life urge and the
paradise that can be accessed when digging for real love. When we
have trouble sorting through the maze of our *own* entangled minds
and hearts, is it any wonder that we end up anxious, depressed, and

scratching our heads when it comes to determining how to play well with others who have similar challenges—particularly those with whom we have the most intimate connections?

French philosopher Gustave Thibon had his own notions of self-belonging:

> Beware of mirages. Do not run or fly away in order to get free; rather dig in the narrow place which has been given you; you will find God there and everything; God does not float on your horizon, he sleeps in your substance. Vanity runs, love digs. If you fly away from yourself, your prison will run with you and will close in because of the wind of your flight; if you go deep down into yourself you will disappear in paradise.

Thibon believed that no matter where we are or what our circumstances in life, we "will find God ... in the narrow place" inside. Instead of constantly looking out and beyond this here and now, gazing into the distance for someone or something to rescue us, he suggests we drop the binoculars and dig in. Plunge deeply into the feelings of fear and insufficiency that cause us to suffer. When we do, the Indwelling God, our Internal Ally, will always emerge to comfort us with love and support—the lasting kind.

The Human Operating System: Drives That Have Kept Us Alive

When I sat down to write *Happily Ever After ... Right Now*, I felt it was time to create a new love story on planet Earth. And in the book, there is a very detailed outline on how to do that successfully. In *Self Belonging*, I want to continue focusing on the importance of implementing practices, many outlined in *Happily,* that support us in letting go of our subconscious strongholds. I believe that engaging in these practices is a basic requirement for creating that new love story. At the hub of our subconscious is a web of conditioning born in our primal past that continues to serve up a cocktail of brain chemicals and neurotransmitters that regulate the systems, organs, and changes in our bodies. When you become aware of the auto-regulated-programming that has been influencing your behavior, you can start to be in charge of creating your own programs.

This fascinating internal combo of brain chemicals and neurotransmitters has been collaborating with the cosmos since time immemorial in a conspiracy to perpetuate the human race. When we're not aware of the impact of this conspiracy on our moods and patterns of behavior, we're often driven to doing things that aren't in our best interest.

Behavioral psychologist B.F. Skinner postulated that our learning and development can be influenced by "predictable consequences." He labeled the interplay of these consequences, or the use of reinforcement to strengthen or diminish behavior, "operant conditioning"—a learning process in which behavior is sensitive to or influenced by circumstances that produce punishment, reward, or extinction (cessation of the behavior). He classified operant conditioning into the following categories:

Neutral operants—neutral responses from the environment that neither increase nor decrease the likelihood of behavior being repeated. For example: An average high school student is relatively dispassionate about her studies and maintains mediocre grades. Her teachers don't comment on her performance, neither praising nor denigrating her studies. Because her teachers appear to be neutral, she isn't motivated to change or work any harder.

HOW CONDITIONING INFLUENCES RELATIONSHIPS

Positive re-enforcement—responses from the environment that increase the probability of behavior being repeated. For example: Another average high school student has to work hard to consistently make A's. When she produces high marks, she's repeatedly praised by her teachers, and this positive re-enforcement motivates her to keep up her efforts.

Punishing or negative re-enforcement—responses from the environment that decrease the probability of behavior being repeated. For example: A third, average high school student makes little effort toward her studies and repeatedly produces failing grades. There's no explanation for her lack of motivation other than her seeming laziness. When she's called to the principal's office on two occasions to discuss her poor performance, once with a surprise appearance by her parents, she perceives the consequence as negative, which motivates her to apply herself more diligently to her studies. The negative reinforcement decreases her chances of staying stuck in patterns of failing grades.

Variable reward: In observing lab mice, Skinner learned that they responded insatiably to rewards that were randomly provided. When the mice pressed a lever, they would sometimes get a small treat, sometimes a large one, and other times no treat at all. The uncertainty motivated the mice to keep pressing the lever, intensifying their desire for the biggest reward—not unlike when people feed slot machines for hours on end, determined to hit the jackpot. Skinner learned from his experiments that of all the re-enforcers of behavior, variable reward was the most powerful.

According to neuroscience, dopamine is a neurotransmitter in the brain influenced by the consequence of pleasurable rewards. However, once the prize has been delivered, the gratification quickly fades as the effects of the reward are temporary. Therefore, unless we have an effective self-regulating system in place, we can be driven to continue seeking that pleasurable feeling. This setup was originally designed to keep us on our toes, in search of food and sex to sustain our lives.

Behavioral cravings (such as for sex) driven by our dopamine systems can be just as powerful as chemically induced cravings (such as for drugs or alcohol) in producing what scientists call dopamine-driven desire. It turns out that we have the same pre-wired instincts for seeking short-term rewards as our ancient ancestors, in spite of the fact that our ancestral brains were driven by survival issues that we no longer face. In a post-modern world with countless options at our disposal, variability—or that random system of rewards discovered by Skinner in his lab—can often be the brain's cognitive nemesis, overriding more evolved tendencies for self-control and moderation.

Piggybacking on Skinner's models, modern educator Linda Hartoonian Almas theorizes that the variable reward phenomenon is one of the reasons people stay in abusive relationships. Getting a hit of pleasure somewhere in the mix of "horrible, horrible, wonderful, mean, mean, horrible, wonderful, horrible, mean, wonderful, wonderful, horrible" is what keeps the seeker going back for more— just like the lab mice. Almas explains that the chance of a wonderful moment with your partner drives some of us to endure the pain of abusive relationships, keeping us stuck in the dopamine-induced lure of the possibility for getting lucky.

Since I, too, have long suspected that variable reward has something to do with people staying in abusive relationships, I found Almas' theory enormously helpful—especially in making sense of my own experience. Had Anastasia Steele from *Fifty Shades of Grey* been a real-life human exposed to this information, my guess is that she would have been able to see beyond those fifty shades.

The compulsions motivated by dopamine-driven desire are functions of our human operating system that have kept us alive for millennia. These drives stirred the arousal of our curiosity, inspiring us to hunt, chase, procreate, and nest into our tribes. But since there are nearly eight billion of us around today, we're no longer an endangered species. Yet, we're still vulnerable to our primal tendencies, ever potent after all these thousands of years. So, in order to avoid being bullied by these tendencies, we have to become *aware* of what we're doing and why.

In our commitment to clear our psyches that are threaded by ancient seeds and modern dilemmas, we can begin by staring down what scares us—particularly the things we're most terrified to see in ourselves. Are you able to tolerate your discomfort—even just a moment longer than you thought you could? If you can, you may notice yourself starting to soften around the hard edges of fear and doubt. That's when the narrow place within is revealed to you. As you continue to dive into this internal river of well-being, you will find at its source your very own open, expansive heart. It's here, in the womb of this heart-space, where you may disappear in paradise.

Women Who Love Too Much

"I had been wandering about in the enchantment of romance, afflicted with the worst female curse on earth, the need to mold myself to expectations," the character of Sarah said in Sue Monk Kid's book, *The Invention of Wings*. Sarah felt restricted by the limits imposed on women in the early 19th century, but I believe this curse—this need to mold ourselves to expectations—is still a common syndrome among women today.

Robin Norwood's book, *Women Who Love Too Much*, was a

torchbearer in the mid-1980s, giving voice and guidance to women who over-function (or do too much) in and for their relationships. A marriage and family therapist, Norwood experienced her own personal crisis, which she attributes in part to the "loving too much syndrome." Those of us with similar tendencies set our senses squarely on the relationship, while often (or always, in some cases) ignoring our own needs and possibly neglecting our life purpose.

But is this love? I don't think so.

What is it then? Is it need, fear of abandonment, longing for security, or wanting to be rescued? Is love in there somewhere? Yes, but it's hidden by the feelings of insufficiency and inadequacy that the female archetype has deeply entrenched in us.

Instead, we must fortify the practices that support us in traveling new pathways—behaviors and responses that accentuate compassion, loving kindness, and forgiveness—starting with ourselves. Then, the powerful forces that drive us to move in our typical ways will diminish. We'll be equipped and more and more at ease in choosing to travel in unfamiliar territory. Those of us who have loved too much must learn step-by-step, inch-by-inch how to self-belong. Eventually, taking new roads will be like drawing breath (meaning literally to *inspire*) as self-belonging becomes our clear and primary path.

The Setup

"Women, for centuries, have been trained into dependency, and men, out of it," according to Judith Viorst in her book, *Necessary Losses*. Therein lies the initial set up, dating back to our earliest origins. Once again, this is described as the curse of our human condition—a blight that she says impacts how men and women interact, particularly when unaware of this curse's potential power.

Why does this happen? The bond between mamma mammal and

her babies stimulates one of the most powerful chemicals on earth—oxytocin—widely known as the "love chemical." This hormone is also a neurotransmitter in the brain. It originated in the female mammal approximately 160 million years ago to promote the bonding of mother and cub. So, it should come as no surprise that love and connection lie at the very heart of a woman's identity—that a woman thrives on intimacy and love, while males typically define themselves by their achievements rather than their connections or attachments. Men are also motivated by their dopamine-driven primal desire to "spread their seed." This desire is complicated by modern society's demands for conformity to the very domestication and monogamy that their ancient wiring resists. If men are to be accepted in a post-modern paradigm, they must find ways to regulate their innate desires.

Carol Gilligan, the famed Harvard psychologist, wrote *In a Different Voice*: "Male and female voices typically speak of different truths, the former of the role of separation as it defines and empowers the self, the latter of the ongoing process of attachment that creates and sustains the human community." It's only because we live in a world where maturity is equated with autonomy, argues Gilligan, that women's concern with relationships appears to be a weakness instead of a strength.

Perhaps it's both. In my research for *Self Belonging*, I came to understand that while both autonomy and individuation are important to growth, studies show that vulnerability, or the willingness to allow yourself to be exposed exactly as you are, is one of the most valuable of human assets. Of course, allowing yourself to be exposed takes courage. And it has been my experience that self-belonging fortifies that courage.

Why, then, do we still so often consider vulnerability to be a weakness, particularly in boys and men?

Alpha Male Training

I will never forget the occasion of my father's funeral when I heard my nephew advise his then nine-year-old son, "You can't cry when you deliver your part of the eulogy" (for his beloved great-grandfather). I stared at the closed casket in front of me that held the remains of my father, as I pondered this stern directive. The whole scene seemed impossibly surreal. I wondered what Dad might be experiencing in another dimension—perhaps expanded beyond his alpha male training that taught him to avoid sappy emotions. What would he feel if he tuned in to the event memorializing his life? Wouldn't he be honored if this young man showed some vulnerability and tenderness when sharing stories about their time together? For that matter, why shouldn't we all be tearful? Even though he was old, his death had been sudden and shocking. The last time any of us had been with this man, he was probably laughing at one of his own jokes.

I didn't speak on my great-nephew's behalf that day. The boy got through his talk without shedding a tear. Did he shut down his emotions? Let's do the math. He idolized the man he was honoring, and he was only *nine*. At the very least, I'm certain this event added to the collection of incidents in his programming to become an alpha male. Sadly, I believe my family to be no different than the norm.

Is this alpha male syndrome, which promotes the repeated squelching of feelings (other than anger), responsible for some of the heinous acts perpetrated in our world today? Is there any heart in war, acts of torture, violence, and abuse? Who will break the chain of the long lineage of alphas in the history of my own family of origin—or in yours?

Rewiring the Circuits

The gender differences highlighted by Gilligan and Viorst are, in essence, examples of Jung's insoluble problems. When I repeatedly succumb to conditioned patterns (insoluble problems), regardless of the consequences—I remain a prisoner of my fear and stay sequestered in that narrow place. In such a state, I either see myself as a victim, villain, or rescuer (as a woman who loves too much). I don't blame myself for falling prey to my tendencies, since they're widely prevalent in the mass consciousness of humanity. But it's still up to me to face and then disarm my inner predator. Once I do, I can then take responsibility for what's going on in my life. And, I wonder, what would happen to the state of humanity if everyone did the same thing?

In most cases, we humans don't set out to hurt ourselves and each other. But we do because of the quagmire of unresolved stuff that sits and stews in our subconscious, primed and ready to bubble up when we're triggered. When we become aware of that propensity *even slightly* in advance of a charge, we can create a little space to possibly step out of the predicament. All that life urge needs is just a breath or two to slip through even the tiniest crack in our consciousness. And maybe, by the sixth or seventh breath, whatever it was that caused the trigger might just start to lose its fizz.

In most cases, we humans don't set out to go haywire by hurting ourselves and each other, but we do.

Gandhi said, "Strength does not come from a physical capacity. It comes from an indomitable will." It definitely takes an indomitable will to overcome some of the influences of our conditioning and habits—but it *can* be done. How do I know? I'm a work in progress with some positive results to show for it.

Viorst, Gilligan, Norwood, and Skinner are guides who can help us understand the challenges and complications of our current human wiring. Their theories and findings offer important clues about why we do what we do. With the benefit of their insights, we have a broader lens to view the complexities of our challenges. Even though we're at the top of the food chain, we're still animals. And theoretically, we could be trained like the mice and rats that are used to study our behavior.

But we're also beings blessed with higher levels of reasoning than other primates, so we have the capacity to self-regulate. But first, we have to become aware of what needs to be regulated. Once we fine-tune our internal antenna, we have a prime opportunity to cultivate the focus, will, and determination to change. While psychotherapy and attending workshops can be helpful, it's primarily about committing to practices that will remap our brain circuitry, guiding us into upgraded states of consciousness.

I believe there are three sequential steps for upgrading into our most optimal potential:

Education. We have to educate ourselves so that we can come to understand why we do what we do, especially when the patterns we perpetuate are dysfunctional.

Awareness. We must be committed to becoming aware of any dysfunction so that we can take steps to change.

Action. We need to cultivate the will and determination to change and then proceed with the exercises and mental focus that will catapult us into the expanded states where we are meant to live.

Our very thoughts and experiences can actually change the structure of our brains through a process known as neuroplasticity.

Fortunately, there is now promising data from scientists and researchers, which shows that with training, we can transcend the effects of our conditioning. Our very thoughts and experiences can actually change the structure of our brains through a process known as neuroplasticity. In the next chapter, I'll also talk about the study of epigenetics, which has shown that genes can be influenced and altered by the environment (including your thoughts), even if the underlying DNA doesn't change.

It may seem like an impossible task to break free from the entangled circuits in our heads. We can ponder things over and over in our minds and be tempted to stay stuck in the story, or we can take advantage of the opportunity for healing and growth. At any moment we can choose to claim our power by walking away from anything that doesn't serve us.

Beyond Conditioning—The Role of Karma in Relationships

To some of you, what I'm about to say will sound outrageous. But my personal belief—the one that makes the most sense to me, is that our souls choose certain circumstances to support our optimal growth and ultimate actualization over many lifetimes and incarnations.

In such a paradigm, we invariably interact with certain souls we have known before in other lifetimes in order to finish business left undone. We confront consequences of actions, words, and deeds—

both ours and theirs—that created a residue, or *karma*, that needs to be cleared for our optimal growth. We clamor to find each other in order to make peace and release ourselves from the past.

In the karmic model, anyone who shows up as your nemesis could just be your greatest teacher. And the two of you may have signed up for your respective roles in order to dissolve karma and expand your soul's potential. Of course, if that's the case, neither party can be seen as a victim or villain, regardless of how things may appear. Maybe that's why the sages advise us to have gratitude for everything—no matter what may seem to be going on.

Tools for Optimizing Potential

Whether or not you adhere to the karmic model, studies show unequivocally that some form of repeated mental training and focus each day can support neuroplasticity—changes in the brain that strengthen healthier ways of being. These practices include yoga, meditation, mindful walking, or even sports—just so long as whatever you are engaged in causes you to focus your attention in the present moment for a period of time each day. With repeated discipline and determination, you'll continue to see results, some subtle and some perhaps profound.

While continuing to strengthen my own practice of meditation, physical workouts, yoga, regular sleep and wake cycles, healthy diet, and mingling social interactions with supportive friends and family, I'm beginning to see glimmers of Gustave Thibon's paradise—deep in the narrow space within.

* Practice *

Heart, Breath, and Gratitude

Sit in a comfortable position. Put your right hand over your heart. As you do, realize that the pumping of this heart of yours is just you and your version of what created you. Watch your breath for a few counts. Acknowledge that you're the only one required in this scenario. For another minute or two, hone in on these unique functions—your beating heart and your breath. If you can, muster up some gratitude and loving kindness for yourself. Practice digging down into the heart and breath of the narrow place within— even if just for two or three minutes a day for a while. It isn't necessary for you to understand what's going on. If you can, just trust the process. Doing so could be the start (or continuation) of your journey toward "disappearing in paradise."

In the next chapter, we'll continue to explore the process of conditioning in the brain and how certain behavioral patterns can form and persist due to subconscious strongholds. We will examine the work of cellular biologist Bruce Lipton, who has shown through his research that our very cells and genetic structure can be altered by our thoughts. And we'll learn how to run our own programs, instead of allowing our unconscious programming to take over.

FOUR

How Happiness Gets Hijacked

*

A Community of the Spirit

There is a community of the spirit.
Join it, and feel the delight
of walking in the noisy street,
and being the noise.

Drink all your passion,
and be a disgrace.

Close both eyes
to see the other eye.

Open your hands,
if you want to be held.
…
Sit down in this circle.

Quit acting life a wolf,
and feel the shepherd's love filling you.

At night, your beloved wanders.
…
Tonight, no consolations.
…
Close your mouth against food,
Taste the lover's mouth in yours.

56

HOW HAPPINESS GETS HIJACKED

You moan, But she left me. He left me.
Twenty more will come.

Be empty of worrying.
Think of who created thought

Why do you stay in prison
when the door is so wide open?

Move outside the tangle of fear-thinking.
Live in silence.

Flow down and down in always
widening rings of being.

—Rumi

The expression "time heals all" isn't what we want to hear when we're suffering from a significant loss.

Adele, the young British sensation who endured a breakup with a man she described as "the love of my life," said in a 2012 *Vogue Magazine* interview that it took her months of living through "a pretty dark period" before she was able to begin to see glimmers of light.

What I continue to understand about this time thing is that it provides an environment for a self-rebooting, helping us to understand that we can live, grow, and flourish *without* whatever we thought we had to have in order to be okay.

First of all, as we heal from a loss or begin to recover from any attachment or addiction, we have to consider what it means to be okay. Or how about going beyond okay-ness into the thriving zone?

If you've been living with an experience that doesn't support you in thriving—something that's eclipsed your magnificence in *any* way—and you've come to recognize the truth of the situation, do you really have a choice of whether or not to let go of it? Even if it feels like you're jumping off a cliff into a very deep, dark abyss, don't you have to take the plunge?

In my case, I wasn't able to develop this material until I let go of my relationship with Richard. After all, I was allowing him to drain my very life force. When I finally released him, I created a space to receive any and all of the nutrients that would nurture the soil for growing myself anew. In other words, I learned how to stop allowing my happiness to be hijacked, so I could enter the thriving zone.

Adele had to do her own letting go and creating space for growth. In February 2012, she swept the GRAMMY Awards with her album and title song, *Rolling in the Deep*, inspired by her breakup. Prior to watching the GRAMMYs, I caught an interview with her in which she shared her compelling story about creating the song with co-writer Paul Epworth, while she was in the depths of emotional despair. Her rise to international celebrity was intrinsically tied to personal agony—a force that ignited the core of her creativity and drove her to unprecedented fame.

Over a period of months, she not only suffered the crisis of her breakup, but also endured a scary vocal hemorrhage, temporarily losing the incredible voice that launched her to stardom. Yet, on stage at the GRAMMYs, she appeared to be fully healed as she crooned the winning song in an unforgettable performance.

How did she do it? How did she heal herself from devastation and despair while simultaneously rising to extraordinary success? My guess is that she gave herself permission to experience her anger and sense of betrayal, which she openly shares in *Rolling in the Deep*. Somewhere along the way, the anger started to lose its grip. The man she had once seen as the villain who betrayed her ultimately played a major role in changing her life. She learned to stop letting that experience hijack her happiness, and her nemesis became her blessing.

When we're willing to fully examine what's behind the visible, raw pain of any challenge, we can begin to unravel the riddle perpetuated by our naiveté and blind spots. Then, we can start to see the secret, shadowy force that needs to be exposed. Once you allow your pain to be fully revealed and you realize you can actually tolerate that revelation, you'll be fully supported in rolling in your own deep and powerful nature. That's the essence of self-belonging.

So how can you support yourself to do something so scary and life-changing? By continuing to realize that it's a better choice than channeling your precious energy and life urge down the rabbit hole of anxiety and despair. If you can just muster the fortitude to take that leap of faith, no matter how frightening, something far better than the mediocrity or misery you've already endured awaits you—guaranteed. How do I know? Remember, I'm your personal research project.

Like Adele, it took me time to grieve and muster the courage to reposition Richard in my mind and heart. I needed to dive into my developing sense of self-belonging and overrule the instincts deeply ingrained in my psyche. I spent hours and days and months uprooting those instincts, and it has absolutely paid off.

Of course, to do this, you have to trust that in the space left by whatever you're releasing, there will be an opportunity for something better that will support your growth, optimal potential, and happiness. While that trust may seem hard to obtain, the alternative means allowing mediocrity, abuse, or something else to eclipse your magnificence. When you do that, you make a declaration to yourself and the Universe that you don't believe you deserve anything but the average, ordinary, or even below-neutral zone.

If you're reading the words on this page, you're meant for a completely different stratosphere beyond those options. You, dear heart, were born to shine, and in order to glow, you have to keep doing whatever it takes to turn up your inner light bulb. As you continue reading, we'll explore more ways for you to do just that.

Happiness Hijacking

Living through several Colorado winters finally convinced me to get my wood-burning fireplace in working order. After doing so, I spent many hours sitting in front of that fireplace, contemplating the flames devouring the wood as it dissolved into molten ash. In watching it all slowly simmer, I was repeatedly guided to consider what might be brewing in my own internal kettle. As we start to crank up those inner light bulbs of ours, isn't learning how to moderate our emotional hot spots integral to the process? I'm clearly a work in progress, as in the course of any given day my own smoldering embers can and do combust.

The following scenario provides an example. There are strict parking regulations in the alpine village where I live, and the fines are steep if you break the rules. One day, my allotted meter time ran out a minute or two before I got to my car. Like an agent in *Minority Report* (the science fiction film about mutants who foresee crime before it occurs), the parking patrol seemed to nail me just as the meter struck zero, slapping a fresh ticket on my windshield. Since this phantom-ticket-man vanished as quickly as he'd appeared, I felt fumes rising from my gut. Fortunately, I took a few breaths, calmed down, and quietly drove away, considering the truth of what had happened. This guy was simply doing his miserable job. Couldn't I just muster up some compassion for him rather than obsessing about my own inconvenience? What would it be like to be the object of repeated disdain from other parking violators?

I thought about what the parking-patrolman and the scene he unwittingly participated in represented in my life. Did I have some anger and rage smoldering in my inner boiler room? What did this man's apparent authority over me and my seeming helplessness provoke?

I came to realize that it wasn't the man or even the situation that had caused my upset. It was the anger I'd projected onto him for his perceived betrayal of me—like I'd done with my father and Richard before him. Simply put, he had triggered my subconscious material.

The parking scenario—like so many other fiascos in life—highlighted the fact that underneath the trigger, and how awful things seemed because of it, the incident also provided a reservoir of information about my inner world. It was another opportunity for me to see what was truly happening within rather than view the situation through the lens of anger and unprocessed pain.

In the opening poem for this chapter, ancient Sufi poet Rumi wrote, "Close both eyes to see the other eye." In closing both eyes, we can use our "internal eye" to see what's hiding inside of us. That process helps us identify the circumstances, people, fears, and beliefs that persuade us away from the path that leads to self-belonging—so that we can let go of anyone or anything that hijacks our happiness.

Examining the Shadow

Carl Jung referred to "the shadow" as the subconscious aspect of the personality. Based on extensive research, Bruce Lipton has said that ninety-five percent of how we operate in the world originates from our subconscious mind, which is a storage tank for conditioning and habits.

So, if we have anger and rage stewing in the shadow/subconscious like I discovered after my parking incident, how likely is it that I can always operate from a state of compassionate, loving-kindness—the sure path to well-being according to Christ and Buddha?

For example, consider the first words that might cross your lips when you crack your head on the cabinet door that someone else left ajar? Might it be to blame that person for leaving the door open rather than to take responsibility for keeping yourself out of harm's way? The next time you experience a similar incident, take note of what happens. Just be *aware* of what occurs without judging yourself. As much as I want to believe that I'm moving into expanded states of consciousness, such as sustained periods of compassion and loving kindness, I'm often astounded at my reaction to that kind of episode or experiences like the one with the parking-patrolman.

In his book, *Healing the Shadow,* Ross Bishop says:

> *After many years of work and study, I have come to the firm belief that there is no independent evil force separate from man's own inner darkness (the shadow). I believe the origin of our darkness is twofold. Part has to do with karma we carry from our unresolved past struggles, and part is from our unresolved childhood wounding. Both of these reside in the "shadow," (per Jung) and if not healed can lead us to inflict great pain upon others and ourselves.*

Jung explained that when our own inner demons are unresolved, we're subconsciously inclined to inflict pain on others. Doing so can bring temporary relief by deflecting the unprocessed pain away from the self. Bishop adds: "This (projection) is the basis for crime, sexual (emotional and physical) abuse, and political and business corruption (among a multitude of other deviant behaviors)." Of course, there are those who would argue that there's an independent, malevolent force (like Satan), which could serve as a convenient excuse for evil-making. But I agree with Bishop and Jung—that subconscious behaviors, driven by habituated patterns, are fundamentally the cause of evil in the world.

So, if we're heavily influenced by our subconscious behavior, how can we become aware of the possible ninety-five percent of ourselves that lives under the radar? To my knowledge, there isn't one, foolproof formula for that leap in awareness. We simply have to be willing to turn and face the perceived predator, whether a parking-patrolman or a sharp kitchen cabinet, and remove the projection to discover what's hiding behind the mask that our inner beast might happen to be wearing.

The Role of the Brain

As we're beginning to see, we all carry hidden agendas, sometimes consciously or creatively, and sometimes hidden under layers of mist. When we decide to look into the fog, the logical place to begin is, of course, the brain. What we find there is fascinating. Deeply complex and utterly magical, the human brain, as now revealed by advanced technology, is a universe in itself.

Joseph LeDoux, neuroscientist and distinguished pioneer in the study of human emotions, has received numerous honors for his research, focused primarily on the biological underpinnings of memory, emotions, and fear. In his breakthrough book, *The Emotional Brain,* LeDoux reminds us that the brain evolved from the back to the front. The back is the limbic system where the amygdala and our emotional centers reside. It's the wanting and fear part, which is approximately 450 million years old and designed for survival. The front or cerebral cortex is a much newer part of our anatomy, wired for reasoning and restraint.

Because the back of the brain is much older, more neuropathways run from the back to the front than vice versa. Therefore, once your emotions are ignited, as in anger at the parking-patrolman, it's difficult to turn those neuropathways off. Even though reasoning and restraint are dialed into the front of our heads (the cerebral cortex), the limbic system can easily overrule the memo from the front that says this man isn't a real danger.

To make matters more complicated, the limbic system reads any threat as the same, no matter where our rational minds rate that threat on a scale of mild to extreme. So as LeDoux explains, for many of us, "emotional arousal dominates and controls thinking." He offers an explanation below:

> *Emotions evolved not as conscious feelings, but as brain states and bodily responses. [These] are the fundamental facts of an emotion.... As things now stand, the amygdala (the part of the limbic system which primarily processes memory and emotion) has a greater influence on the cortex (where the higher levels of reasoning are located), than the cortex has on the amygdala. Although thoughts can easily trigger emotions (by activating the amygdala), we are not very effective at willfully turning off emotions (by deactivating the amygdala through using the higher powers of reasoning in the cortex). Telling yourself you should not be anxious or depressed does not help much once your emotions have been activated.*

LeDoux points out that the goal is to continue finding methods for calming the effects of the limbic system when it has gone off on an emotional rampage. He emphasizes that resolving the struggle between thought and emotion doesn't necessarily require that the front of the brain dominate the back. Instead, the hope is to continue finding ways to *balance* the function of both to become complementary to each other. Therefore, the question becomes how can we learn to create a more harmonious balance between reason and passion?

Kahlil Gibran, legendary author of *The Prophet*, offers the following passage on creating such a balance:

> *Your reason and your passion are the rudder and the sails of your seafaring soul. If either your sails or your rudder be broken, you can but toss and drift, or else be held at a standstill in mid-seas. For reason, ruling alone, is a force confining; and passion, unattended, is a flame that burns to its own destruction. Therefore let your soul exalt your reason to the height of passion, that it may sing; And let it direct your passion with reason, that your passion may live through its own daily resurrection.*

Then there's David Wilcock, researcher of consciousness science, who says, "Telling the truth relaxes the nervous system" in his book, *The Source Field Investigations*. Bruce Lipton agrees: "The soul, which does not lie, is the balancing force of the subconscious." So, if the soul has the code to unlock the subconscious, and telling the truth relaxes the nervous system—could being honest and aware about what's *really* going on inside of us be a way to balance reason and passion? From my experience, one sure way to continue being honest and aware is to go into your own ground of self-belonging and learn to truly know yourself there. Speaking for myself, it's a key way I've experienced a daily resurrection. It's how I've reduced the hijacking of my happiness and entered the thriving zone:

> *There is an extraordinary state of well-being which*

exists within each and every one of us. It is an authentic and enduring state of serenity, happiness, wisdom, and freedom. It is the crowning achievement of human development which is gained through inner development and the expansion of consciousness. The ancient Greeks called this Eudaimonia. In modern times we call this human flourishing.

So, says Elliott Dacher, a physician and expert on Integral Medicine and Human Flourishing. Dacher's description captures what I believe to be the essence of self-belonging. He cautions us, however, that: "Whether in the form of materialism, sensory excitement, the quest for romantic intimacy, fame, name, or worldly success" we can get off track and be perpetually diverted from "the real thing." In other words, if we stay stuck at the pit of our brain, we can be lured by the persuasive quick fix to satisfy our life urge. This immediate gratification includes external, temporary solutions like drugs, sex, work, or the romantic ideal. But if we are persuaded in that direction, won't the torment of our longing persist and even keep escalating? Yes. In surfing the top of the wave, we'll almost certainly fail to see the vast ocean of possibilities waiting for us beneath the surface.

How can we get back on the path to self-belonging and the thriving zone if we've taken an outermost detour—like I did when I returned to Richard? Perhaps the new field of epigenetics can give us more of a clue.

Epigenetics and Consciousness

Bruce Lipton has produced breakthrough studies at Stanford University's School of Medicine that show how a single cell's environment influences its behavior and physiology, even to the extent of determining whether or not genes will be activated. His discoveries, which run counter to the established scientific view that all life is controlled by genetic propensity, sanctioned one of today's most important fields of research, the science of epigenetics.

Epigenetics is the study of variations in the cells caused by external or environmental factors that switch genes off and on.

This new science is the study of changes in gene activity that are governed by cellular material known as the epigenome. According to recent research, these epigenetic markers can and do alter gene expressions through environmental influences, suggesting that environment can play a key role in how things unfold in your life.

Bruce Lipton's research has strengthened his understanding of the mind/body connection and how a positive environment cultivated within the mind (such as through meditation or optimistic thinking) can improve health and emotional well-being. In his lectures, he talks about how to use awareness and focus to address habituated patterns in the subconscious mind. When we do, we can learn to be in charge of our own programs rather than serve as pawns on the virtual chessboard of our subconscious.

Lipton's theories provide us with links to our own software so that we can amplify awareness of our thoughts and the behaviors that result. These links may be components in the gradual upgrade of our entire systems, bridges to expanded consciousness, and tools for creating balance between reason and passion.

Science and the Upgrade

As mentioned earlier, Joseph LeDoux has suggested that the amygdala over-functioning-dilemma can be resolved by balancing the pathways that weave back and forth between the back and the front of the brain. I was introduced to LeDoux's work by Geshe Lobsang Tenzin Negi, whom I was privileged to meet in 2006. Lobsang and His Holiness the Dalai Lama are cofounders of the Emory (University) Tibet Partnership formed in 1998. They have since developed a program called Cognitively Based Compassion Training, or CBCT, which is currently being examined in a number of research studies, including a project funded by the National Institute of Health. These studies are investigating the efficacy of compassion meditation on the experience of depression.

CBCT is a method for cultivating well-being through the use of reflective practices, based on centuries-old techniques from the Indo-Tibetan tradition. Taken from the *Lojong* tradition, these practices are designed to bring about "thought transformation." Lobsang and his team have so far been able to show that the regular practice of compassion meditation significantly reduces blood cortisol (stress hormone) levels. The production of cortisol is stimulated by the amygdala (in the limbic system), the "home" of our emotions.

Richard Davidson, Professor of Psychology and Psychiatry at the University of Wisconsin, who earned his doctorate from Harvard University, currently heads up the Center for Healthy Minds at the UW. Their research is focused on cortical and sub-cortical substrates of emotion and affective disorders, including depression and anxiety. A major component of his current work involves the interactions between the prefrontal cortex and the amygdala in the regulation of emotion. He has continued to develop these studies since he began his own collaborations with His Holiness the Dalai Lama in 1992.

At the Dalai Lama's request and encouragement, Davidson has also launched a research project using a team of scientists to investigate the effects of compassion meditation. Experienced meditators from India, Bhutan, and Nepal (people who have practiced for ten thousand hours or more) have been imported to Davidson's lab, where their brains are scanned by functional MRIs (fMRIs) during their meditation practices.

These studies have consistently shown that during meditation, the left prefrontal cortex (together with the anterior cingulate cortex, which we'll discuss in Chapter Six) becomes more active. At the same time, the activity in the amygdala is diminished. As LeDoux suggested, striking this kind of balance in the brain's activity is key to managing our emotions.

Finally, one of the most exciting breakthroughs involving science and the human upgrade has to do with the study of neuroplasticity or the brain's ability to reorganize itself, as I discussed earlier. We know through the science of epigenetics that the environment can alter gene expressions. The study of neuroplasticity takes us one step further, theorizing that the brain can change its own structure and function through thought and activity. There are currently documented cases of people blind since birth who have begun to see, stroke victims incapacitated for years who have moved into recovery, people whose IQ's increased, learning disorders completely overcome, and people with previously incapacitating thoughts and obsessions totally cured — all through neuroplasticity treatments.

In *Ageless Body, Timeless Mind*, a decade before the concept of neuroplasticity was even discussed in scientific communities, Deepak Chopra shared studies demonstrating that environmental influences could reverse some signs and symptoms of aging.

Empowering your Happiness Potential

There are many theories about why we are the way we are—why we suffer, why we can't get a better grip on our lives (even when we try *really* hard), and why it's so difficult to lose a deep love, whether through betrayal, death, or some other form of perceived abandonment. Not unlike me, you've probably been triggered by what can seem to be a trite happening such as my parking-patrol-debacle.

Here's the good news: Even though the process of meeting your pain—whatever your method— can be tedious and challenging, it works. I can fully attest to that. I know it professionally, and I know it personally. Once you dive into the core of it, you realize that your itch or your issue is rarely about any one particular person or any one situation. Instead, you're confronting a pattern of behavior, called to your attention with someone or something's assistance. Having been awakened to that pattern, however inconvenient or painful it may feel at the time, you can identify the source right under your own skin.

It's up to you to *be aware* and recruit the courage to examine what's really going on. As you continue processing the event and any accompanying pain it has caused, notice that you're gradually creating more distance between you and whatever provoked you. Eventually, the stronger life urge will take precedent, the issue at hand will continue losing its urgency, and the life force will support you in transcending any tendencies that will overrule your potential for happiness.

Meditation

Meditation is the practice of cultivating self-understanding. It is an opportunity to release all that doesn't serve and open to the love, light, and joy that you truly are.

HOW HAPPINESS GETS HIJACKED

—Eaden Shantay

Professors Davidson and Lobsang are two of many who are doing research to show that meditation (mental focus) absolutely brings the brain and blood into better balance, supporting us in creating more distance between our emotions and our responses to them. Below is a practice for the form of compassion meditation (CBCT) shown by current research to be effective in reducing cortisol levels in the blood and balancing several chemicals in the brain.

Compassion Meditation: Fifteen minutes

The experts on this meditation continue to emphasize the main focus of this exercise—that all beings share something in common. We want to be happy. And if you participate in contributing to your own happiness as well as others'—even for those you most resist—by holding compassion in your heart for all, then you will have contributed to raising the human ocean of consciousness every single time you engage in this practice.

* Practice *

Sit comfortably. Breathe in and out five times. Bring to mind people whom you love and for whom you already have compassion. Include yourself in this group. Keep these people in mind for three to five minutes, while repeatedly sending them thoughts of love and compassion.

Next, consider a group of people with whom you are acquainted but only superficially. You feel pretty neutral about them. Again, ponder the group for three to five minutes with compassionate thoughts.

Finally, bring to mind people you resist—even those you feel have betrayed you. Do your best to send them compassion too.

Contemplate engaging in this practice for thirty days. At the end of the month, see if you notice any changes in how you respond to life. At the end of your practice, you may wish to include the following:

Loving Kindness Meditation/Intention

May all beings be free from hatred, anger, jealously, stress, and suffering. May all beings experience peace, well-being, and happiness.

In the next chapter, we will explore the history of our biology and how it continues to influence our current behaviors, drives and attachments, while continuing to recognize the importance of waking up to our patterns—particularly the ones that keep us sequestered and stuck.

FIVE

Conscious Evolution: Becoming a Game Changer

*

Checkmate

Borrow the beloved's eyes.
Look through them and you'll see the beloved's face
everywhere. No tiredness, no jaded boredom.
"I shall be your eyes and your hand and your loving."
Let this happen and things that
you have hated will become helpers.

A certain preacher always prays long and with enthusiasm
for thieves and muggers who attack people
on the road. "Let your mercy, Oh, Lord, cover their inso-
lence."
He doesn't pray for the good,
but only for the blatantly cruel.
Why is this? His congregation asks.

"Because they have done me such generous favors.
Every time I turn back toward the things they want.
I run into them. They beat me and leave me nearly dead
in the road, and I understand, again, that what they want
is not what I want. They keep me on the spiritual path.
That's why I honor them and pray for them."
Those that make you return, for whatever reason
to God's solitude, be grateful to them.
Worry about the others who give you
delicious comforts that keep you from prayer.

73

SELF BELONGING

Friends are enemies sometimes, and enemies friends.

There is an animal called an ushghur, a porcupine.
If you hit it with a stick, it extends its quills
and gets bigger. The soul is a porcupine,
made strong by stick beating.

So a prophet's soul is especially afflicted
because it has to become so powerful.
A hide is soaked in tanning liquor and becomes leather.
If the tanner didn't rub in the acid
the hide would become foul-smelling and rotten.

The soul is a newly skinned hide, bloody and gross.
Work on it with manual discipline,
and the bitter tanning acid of grief,
and you will become lovely and strong.

If you can't do this work yourself, don't worry.
You don't even have to make a decision
one way or another. The Friend, who knows
a lot more than you do, will bring difficulties,
and grief and sickness, as medicine, as happiness,
as the essence of the moment when you're beaten,
when you hear Checkmate, and can finally say,
with Hallaj's voice,
I trust you to kill me.

-Rumi

Checkmate: Game Over—Radical Responsibility— Radical Compassion

A human being has so many skins inside, covering the depths
of the heart. We know so many things, but we don't know

74

CONSCIOUS EVOLUTION: BECOMING A GAME CHANGER

ourselves! Why, thirty or forty skins or hides, as thick and hard as an ox's or bear's, cover the soul. Go into your own ground and learn to know yourself there.

—Meister Eckhart

Rumi was a 13th century poet who lived in Persia, where chess was played in the Muslim world before spreading to Southern Europe. Currently one of the most widely read poets in America, he was also a Sufi mystic. (The God of the Sufi is considered to be the Divine Presence within.)

Sufis routinely participate in practices and traditions that focus on inner transformation through self-reflection and contemplation. Rumi's poetry, mirroring the influences of Sufi-mysticism, frequently appears to be about accessing various ways to connect to the "Beloved" by letting down defenses and removing the "hides covering the heart." He challenges us to go beneath the surface to seek a deeper meaning to what's happening in our lives, particularly during tough times. Richard Rohr, a Franciscan priest and globally recognized author and speaker, says that a mystic is: "one who has moved from mere belief systems to actual inner experiences of the Divine."

In "Checkmate," Rumi refers to Mansur Al-Hallaj, who was also a Sufi mystic with many followers. (Hallaj lived in the late 800s, so he was Rumi's predecessor.) Hallaj openly communicated his philosophy through his writings and public speaking—often traveling to distant lands, including India and China, in a quest to reach and help people of all ideologies. He would make bold public statements such as "I am the truth" or "There is nothing here but God." His contemporaries objected to his insistence on sharing mysticism with the masses. Eventually, he was tried, imprisoned, and executed for his "crimes" as a heretic.

Like Rumi, German philosopher, Christian mystic, and Dominican priest, Meister Eckhart also lived in the 13th century. His sermons seem to echo Rumi's prose, as when he said: "We will journey into God as we journey into ourselves." Eckhart spoke endlessly on love and compassion and also asserted that God is not a separate being. He said that God is within as God is without. Like Hallaj, Eckhart was tried as a heretic, though he died before he was sentenced. Were Hallaj, Rumi, and Eckhart playing God, or were they simply recognizing the God potential in themselves and in all beings?

With all of this in mind, what message do you think Rumi was trying to impart in *Checkmate*? What does it mean to "see through the eyes of the beloved?" If we put ourselves in alignment with God, surrendering to Divine will, would we focus on competition, wanting to conquer and win? Would we worry about the disgrace of being checkmated?

If we saw others through the "eyes of the beloved," how would they look? Would we concentrate on their imperfections, or would we see them as flawless creations of sacred handiwork? And what did Rumi mean when he said, "I trust you to kill me"? Did Hallaj know on some level when he faced execution that he couldn't really be beaten? Were the ones who killed him (his enemies) really his friends—those who kept him on the spiritual path? And while on that path, seeing through the "eyes of the beloved," would he have worried about being checkmated, suffering humiliation by losing the game, or even dying?

In Chapter Four, we learned from neuroscientist Joseph LeDoux that emotional arousal (fear, anger, etc.), originates in the limbic system and overrides reasoning and restraint. Once fear and anger arise from the back of the brain, the amygdala releases cortisol, powering the fight or flight response, igniting an urge for competition, and sweeping aside compassion, which is processed in a specific region of the cerebral cortex called the anterior cingulate cortex or ACC. In moments of fury, the rational mind—including the ACC—is basically hijacked, while the limbic system manipulates our actions to preserve the species. Or so it thinks.

If we want to replace survival programming with the life urge as our guiding influence—if we want to see through the eyes of the beloved instead of acting as pawns on a chessboard—doesn't it serve us to become aware of how our conditioned behavior may be manipulating us? In this chapter, we'll bring another part of the limbic system into our discussions (mentioned in Chapter Three) that stimulates dopamine-driven desire. Rather than turning exclusively to scholars and science at this point, we'll meet a few couples (human and otherwise) to illustrate the effects of this neurotransmitter in action.

The Limbic System and Pleasure Programming

In an intriguing segment of the *Discovery Channel* series entitled *The Frozen Planet*, a male polar bear was in pursuit during the spring mating season. Happily, he picked up the scent of a female, but he had to travel ten miles to get to her. Once his rugged journey was complete, the trials in reaching his destination looked to be well worth the trouble. He and his potential mate were seen on film engaging in a flirtatious encounter.

Because our polar bear goddess appeared to be the only candidate for mating within a radius of several miles, she pretty much held all of the power—at least as it pertained to when she and our hero bear would connect. She didn't appear to be at all concerned that her male counterpart was twice her size. Instead, she conveyed a quiet confidence and seemed to delight in her coquettish maneuvering as he willingly followed.

Finally, she consented to consummating their relationship. Except not far off on the icy landscape was another hunter, who also picked up on our fair maiden's scent. He, too, surely recognized the scarcity of female companionship and was willing to go to the mat (snow) to win her paw. Nonetheless, our hero bear successfully tackled his challenger, suffering barely a scratch, and proudly sauntered away in arrogant triumph. Unfortunately, he was soon to encounter additional contenders trekking in from all corners, steadfast in the power of their desires.

At the end of the two-week mating period, after fending off all other challengers and winning his lass, our hero was seen limping across the snow-packed terrain. He was severely wounded, battered, and bloodied. He'd been fueled by the fire of competition—a relentless, instinctual dance between his survival brain and the reward centers inside his limbic system, where the amygdala, king of emotional arousal and dopamine-driven desire, resides. Yet, despite all the intensity of the hero bear's desire to be with his polar goddess—and everything he was willing to put himself through in order to win her— in the end, all he could think about was taking off to find some lunch.

I realize I'm anthropomorphizing this polar bear romance, but there are some strikingly familiar chords to their little love fest. In the beginning, the female bear knew instinctively who was the biggest, baddest of them all, and she went right for him. Were her urges eons away from my own? I have always bid for the most handsome, powerful, successful man—the one seen in social circles as a winner. Unlike the bear, of course, I hung on beyond two weeks, perhaps ignoring some political details irrelevant to an animal in the wild. That said, the nuances of her behavior suggest she would never put up with misconduct for one nanosecond. And given everything at stake for the male bear, I doubt that misbehaving would have crossed his mind.

In other words, what our bears lacked in higher reasoning was offset by a simple script and unquestionable choices. Theirs were natural rhythms—no digital clocks ticking anywhere in sight.

The Biological Clock

Then, there's my friend, Lucy, who in her late thirties, worried that *her* hero bear, Brad, would head for the hills before helping to execute her biological agenda. She wanted to make certain she would conceive a child before her ticker had tocked. The couple had been together for a little over two years and had always seemed to enjoy a happy, healthy connection.

Upon my arrival for a visit one day, Lucy shared her concern that Brad appeared distant and unavailable. The more she discussed her concerns, the more she became unhinged—worried that he was going to leave her. I was intimately familiar with that flavor of fear.

Brad eventually told her that he did indeed want to be with her—just not under contract and not if he had to be glued to the bedroom to help her make a baby.

Meanwhile, no matter how Lucy tried to focus on other things, like her promising career, all she could think about was marrying Brad and starting a family. When she felt him pulling away, she started to unravel.

This woman is not only intelligent and wise, but she has a chance to make a real difference with her work. Why couldn't she get a grip? It appeared that her limbic system had eclipsed all reasoning.

In my own case, long after I'd had children who not only filled my heart but satisfied my biological agenda, I faced another limbic dilemma. Even while Richard offered me the "generous favor" of showing some of his precarious tendencies early on, I stayed anyway. Why did I do this? We've looked at a range of possibilities—

subconscious patterns, ancestry, conditioning, karma, and dopamine-driven desire. Was I seduced by variable reward—even when my higher centers of reasoning were screaming at me to scram? Looking through the lens of reason now with some considerable time and distance between Richard and me, it certainly seems possible that the persuasive power of dopamine-driven desire was influential.

Pondering Our Development

Here is something interesting to consider: During the gestation period of about 260 days, Homo sapiens actually go through the entire evolution of all species ever to exist. We start out as a single cell, which has been fertilized by one of a zillion tadpole-looking organisms (the word "sperm" derives from the Greek word meaning "seed"). In a very short period (shorter than any other living species), the single cell begins to multiply. Soon, a creepy-looking creature with a big head appears (looking something like a tadpole), eventually taking on a mammalian appearance (a little more manageable to the eye), and then ultimately emerging as a cuddly little human.

Given this developmental sequence—each stage building on the previous one—it would seem logical that the parts within us from the beginning (like the reptile) don't evaporate when we morph into our human selves. So, even when your precious little pumpkin eventually emerges human, she's still part amphibian. And among the assortment of stuff stirring in her species stew is the limbic system, located just above the reptilian brain and brain stem. This oldest part of the brain is shared by every reptile, fish, amphibian, bird, and mammal. It's interconnected with the brain's reward center, playing a vital role in the high experienced in sexual pleasure.

Here again is what seems to be the cosmic conspiracy—in order to keep us evolving and developing, this fascinatingly complex system

CONSCIOUS EVOLUTION: BECOMING A GAME CHANGER

motivates us with *rewards*. As discussed in Chapter Three, variable reward increases resistance to extinction by rewarding us for keeping that itch, yearning, craving, curiosity, or desire alive—even when our rational centers of reasoning advise us against doing so. Again, those rational centers don't carry much weight when the older part of the brain decides to flex its muscle.

Conditioning can stimulate a certain craving, but not the kind that causes us to discover our dharma or life purpose (discussed at the beginning of Chapter Two). This craving can take precedence over the quiet voice of yearning planted in the depths of our soul that inspires our creativity and passions. The quiet yearning is a different kind of longing than the primal type.

The multitude of quick fixes that will resolve primal urges—as in sex, sugar, drugs, drinks, material possessions, etc.—are all external distractions with temporary effects. Each has the potential for stimulating a flood of feel-good dopamine to all the receptor sites in our heads. And as evidenced by the plight of the hunter and hunted in our polar bear saga, the prize (while extraordinary in the moment) *doesn't last*. Nevertheless, the memory of how that momentary bliss felt is branded in our brain, so we want it again and again. Remember, the limbic system is wired for desire. Logical reasoning, processed in the prefrontal cortex, doesn't yet have the chutzpah to flag us when overruled by the chemical cocktail. The polar bear story is a telling example.

Shortly after my visit with Lucy, I happened to be in a conversation with friends I'll call Doug and Kim. Doug, happily single in his mid-forties, bragged that being male was an advantage because he didn't have a biological clock. (He also happens to be an incredible hunk with no scarcity of female admirers.) The dialogue happened after Kim's revelation that she'd given her boyfriend an ultimatum: either he would marry her, or she'd change course in pursuit of someone who would. (Doug didn't seem at all interested in throwing his hat in the ring.)

Once again, we have a woman who's intelligent, beautiful, accomplished, and fully capable of taking care of herself. Yet, she's hell-bent on getting married and having a baby before her biological ticker fizzles out. Doug, on the other hand, in his self-proclaimed prime at forty-something, appears totally unconcerned about finding a mate and making babies (unlike our polar bear). Even so, I can say with reasonable certainty (all due respect to Doug), that he's likely an active, perhaps subconscious participant in the hunter-chase paradigm—just with slightly different goals in mind than the bear.

We could cite multiple examples of how we're a sophisticated lot—expanded well beyond our polar bear neighbors. Have we come to a point in our evolution when there are other things in our lives to consider besides perpetuating the species and reinforcing our reward centers?

If we really take a deep look at what is going on inside these heads of ours, why wouldn't we want to sustain a substantial supply of do-pamine? On some level, it makes sense to keep that sweet chemical in the coffers. Even so, watching that polar bear go from one pain/pleasure cycle to the next was a vivid wake-up call for me, reminding me of cycles I want to avoid perpetuating in my life. "The things I have hated" (many described in this book) have most certainly helped me to see the truth. And by learning to look through the eyes of the beloved, I realize that when I allow myself to be run by fear and bondage, my behavior is rooted in ancient, primal programming.

Love or Codependent Heaven?

We discussed the women who love too much syndrome in Chapter Three, where I said that women who focus heavily on their relationships (myself included) aren't acting solely out of love. Is there an element of dependency or learned helplessness in the mix? Are women, despite our advances, covertly or overtly trained into this dependency through blatant or subliminal messages downloaded in our developmental years, then strengthened by the limbic system and ancestral influences? As for men, do they have issues with dependency as well, albeit with a slightly different zest?

T. S. Eliot, arguably the most important English language poet of the 20th century, suffered from depression and an unhealthy marriage. In an article in *The New Yorker,* the problem in his marriage was described as "an asphyxiating mutual dependency." Simply put, codependency is when both people are dependent on the other in an unhealthy way. Typically, one person over-functions and tries to fix things, while the other is more detached and focused on some type of addiction (work, rage, drugs, alcohol, drama, etc.). I believe that my relationship with Richard was a classic example of asphyxiating mutual dependency.

A few years ago, I accompanied a friend on a long road trip to help her retrieve her belongings. She was divorcing a man she'd once described as "enlightened." After my first encounter with the guy, I had to force myself to remember two cardinal rules: "do no harm" (borrowed from the Buddhists), and "don't judge" (adopted from the Christians). I have to say, this situation tested me in staying true to both.

Fortunately, I was able to focus my attention on supporting my friend in getting the hell out of town with some of her stuff. Once home in my cozy, safe space, I reflected on the experience. I had to be honest with myself. Her actions had not been so different from my own. Perhaps this "prophet" of hers had given her "the bitter tanning acid of grief" to help her to "become lovely and strong through stick beating." I knew all about that "stick beating" stuff. And in allowing it to happen, I hadn't used a shred of reason, regardless of what I'd accumulated in the way of wits and wisdom. The adventure with my dear friend, for which I am sincerely grateful, added valuable insight in going forward on this self-belonging journey of mine.

The Love Channel

My friend's plight got me thinking: Are we a species who truly knows how to love, or are we shackled by chains of dependency that stifle the brilliance of love? As if our own primal urges are not enough to deal with, are we spellbound by a culture addicted to the byproducts of romance? I invite you to hit any of the "Love" channels on satellite radio and see where you land. Your assignment: listen to six songs in a row (it will take fortitude). You might hear Sting pleading for a lover's loyalty in "If I Ever Lose My Faith in You," followed by another passionate appeal for her undying devotion in "Mad About You." Peter Gabriel sings an ode of complete union reaching heavenly heights in his classic "In Your Eyes." The video for that song has been watched more than 1.2 million times on YouTube.

Then, there's the classic, "I Will Wait for You," by Michelle Grand, Jacques Demy, and Norman Gimbel—an ode to an endless romantic vigil reaching over thousands of years. Really? You'll shape a life waiting for him or her, forgetting all about who *you* are and what *you* came here to contribute? Carly Simon and Michael McDonald wrote "You Belong to Me," amassing a whopping 489,000+ YouTube hits. How about belonging to yourself, letting him belong to himself, and seeing where sweet freedom takes you?

Speaking of which, not every song plays to our limbic frequencies. I'm finally beginning to absorb the essence of Michael McDonald's passion when he belted out the song "Sweet Freedom" with 2.5 million hits on YouTube at this writing.

As your personal research project, I'm fully convinced that this state of freedom is the way we were born to live. How can we let go of our traumas and dramas and just allow the mystery of true love to unfold? Won't it inevitably show up when we dive down into that narrow place, where creativity and truth are written so clearly into our personal dharma codes?

The Love Hormone

If dopamine is the theme song for the love channel, then oxytocin might be Michael McDonald's muse. Oxytocin is the love hormone, which at nearly 300 million years younger than the limbic system, often serves to soften some of its effects. Originating in mammals about 160 million years ago, it helps bond mothers to their offspring. Also dubbed the hug hormone, cuddle chemical, and moral molecule, oxytocin is released during hugging, touching, and orgasm in both sexes. In the brain, it generates aspects of social recognition and bonding, and it may stimulate generosity and trust.

Before mammals (and oxytocin) came into being, our predecessors were running around trying to kill whatever got in the way of them and their dinner—the origin of competition? So, for three quarters of the evolution of life on this planet, creatures were not concerned with anything but survival—how to compete, conquer (checkmate), and kill—all basic to perpetuating themselves through lineage. With the advent of oxytocin, the budding possibility of love was born, heralding new prospects into our mix of human development.

Recall the drama of the polar bears—driven by the male's initial chase, sweetened by moments of flirtatious infatuation, followed by the honey pot competition, and finished by his speedy exit out. Not much cuddle chemical in evidence there. It's obvious that we've moved a bit beyond this dynamic in our human form—but only slightly, in my opinion. The hunter/chase/whose-gonna-win-the-game syndrome as played out by our polar bears is actually still alive and well in our own species. If you don't believe me after being in co-dependent heaven on the love channel, take a look at the Hollywood dramas glaring at you in the grocery store checkout line. Do we idolize the stars and crave to know their every movement off-screen? With all the press they receive about their personal lives, it would appear to be so.

How can we move into the "sweet freedom" of real love? Oxytocin is a force and, potentially, an inspiration. Just dial up Steve Winwood next time for his post-limbic prayer-song, "Higher Love."

Winning the Game Or Becoming the Prophet?

The annual Super Bowl is the most watched television show in the United States. Of course, this is a football game, which is an aggressive, sometimes violent sport often involving injuries to players, occasionally severe and even life-threatening. A few stagger off the field—sometimes carried away "bloodied and gross," all for the sake of winning—not unlike our hero bear. Now in the case of football, the triumph doesn't seem to be about getting into the honey pot, although I have no doubt it has been a bonus on many a victorious occasion. The perks for being the biggest, baddest dudes who win the Super Bowl are money, power, and prestige.

I harbor no personal ill will towards football. My two sons are enthralled with the game. I don't care if people play football, like football, or become die-hard fans. I just don't want to be one of them. Does my lack of interest in football exemplify a sexual split in the limbic system? Certainly, many women like football, but I venture to guess more than a few might be in my camp. Stereotypes aside, I actually find basketball a slightly more civilized game. While still an aggressive, competitive sport, it's at least played in a temperature-controlled environment. I once watched The University of Kentucky defeat The University of Kansas (my alma mater) in the National Championship basketball tournament. With the final score tallied, there was nothing but gleeful triumph glowing in the sparkly smiles of the winners, while my homeys, checkmated, quietly sauntered off the court, heads tucked and spirits broken — until the next season, when the entire primal cycle starts all over.

What is it that continues to fuel our competitive nature — the compelling force that keeps coaxing us to escape defeat at all costs — to avoid being checkmated? Are instincts, rooted in our primal past, thwarting our conscious evolution? Are we still preoccupied with the winning (and losing) game rather than focusing on how we can contribute to transcending nihilism and negativity for the greater good of all?

As a woman, I take responsibility for having played many roles, none of which may have actually represented who I really am.

How can I continue my own process of conscious evolution (even in the midst of all this competition), and recognize the moment when I'm hit with the stick, like the ushghur in Rumi's poem? When do I get bigger and extend my quills, and when do I choose to step back and assess how I'm showing up in the world? How can I consciously connect with others who are asking the same questions? One path for me is to research and write this book, which is my way of having that "conversation with the world" noted in the beginning poem in Chapter One. I know you have your own ideas on how to support conscious evolution, and I believe that together, we can use those ideas to be game-changers.

As a woman, I take responsibility for having played many roles, none of which may have actually represented who I really am. I acknowledge the times I've felt fear and desperation in the face of perceived abandonment. In the paralysis of that feeling, I've compromised myself and my integrity in order to avoid being left. I've made choices that often barred my growth and even turned the key at times, locking myself into my own self-imposed cage.

Notes to Myself on Transcending the Self-Imposed Cage

Worry less. Love more.

Realize I have the key to my self-imposed cage. Unlock the door.

Walk through.

Have faith.

Tell the truth to myself about what's going on.

Tell the truth with discernment to others.

Avoid righteousness.

Have gratitude for something every day. Start with your eyesight.

See through the "eyes of the beloved" when you're looking in the mirror.

See through the "eyes of the beloved" when looking at others (all of them).

Realize there are no victims, so you can't be one.

Realize there are no villains, so forgive your perceived betrayers.

Forgive yourself (if there aren't any villains, you can't be one either).

Have compassion and tolerance for yourself.

Have compassion and tolerance for others—even the ones you resist.

Be able to see that your pain is your potion. Let the things you have hated become helpers.

Quit taking things personally. People are just doing what they do. Their actions are almost never about you. Correction: Their actions are never about you.

Trust the "friend, who knows a lot more than you."

Reflections on Richard

Twenty years ago, prior to writing *Happily Ever After ... Right Now*, I had a dream, which was the inspiration for the book. In that dream, I was walking toward a lake banked in mountains in a place unfamiliar to me in waking life. I was completely alone, yet I felt unparalleled love. It was everywhere—above, below, beside, and inside. I can still feel that state of love today and have finally come to realize that in continuing to learn the art of self-belonging, the love I felt in that dream was being *generated from my own heart*. This love was all-inclusive. Everyone was a part of it—even the "thieves and muggers."

Ever since that prophetic dream of mine, I have wanted to be an active participant in co-creating a new love story on planet Earth. Richard's presence in my life supported me in removing the skins and hides that had covered my heart. The bitter tanning acid of grief was the medicine that cranked up my internal oxytocin supply, activating my love hormones.

89

It turns out that as your personal research project, I'm continuing to learn first-hand the power in the messages of the mystics, some of whom literally died for love. They have given us the perfect antidote for whatever may be going haywire in our heads—overactive limbic system and all. With their guidance, I'm learning how my heart can swallow up this head of mine—just like in the dream.

My relationship with Richard was about me finally understanding that the things I had hated have become helpers. By looking through the eyes of the beloved, both in the mirror and in my mind's eye at Richard, I clearly see how he was a gift in my life. My adventures with Richard cleared my path to freedom, providing kindling to build a fire in my heart and ignite the engine that would catapult me out of my self-imposed cage—for good. What jimmies the lock? Trying to let anything but love slip through.

"Freedom" from *The Untethered Soul*

If you sit within the Self, you will experience the strength of your inner being even when your heart feels weak. This is the essence of the path. This is the essence of a spiritual life. Once you learn that it is okay to feel inner disturbances, and that they can no longer disturb your seat of consciousness, you will be free. You will begin to be sustained by the inner energy flow that comes from behind you. When you have tasted the ecstasy of the inner flow, you can walk in this world and the world will never touch you. That is how you become a free being—you transcend.

—*Michael Singer*

CONSCIOUS EVOLUTION: BECOMING A GAME CHANGER

Meditation: Sitting in the Self

Many of those doing research on the benefits of meditation, including Professors Davidson and Lobsang, say that if we're going to accomplish a balance between the limbic system and prefrontal cortex, *we have to exercise our will to stabilize the mind.* Andrew Newberg, physician of nuclear medicine and adjunct professor of Religious Studies at the University of Pennsylvania, co-wrote *How God Changes the Brain*, a book based on brain-scan studies of meditators and the influence of spiritual belief on the brain itself. The authors note:

> *When you intensely and consistently focus on your spiritual values and goals, you increase the blood flow to your frontal lobes and anterior cingulate cortex, which causes activity in emotional centers to decrease. Conscious attention is the key, and the more you focus on your inner values, the more you can take charge of your life.*

* Practice *

Return to the practice in Chapter Three—"Heart, Breath, and Gratitude"—while sitting within the Self, experiencing the strength of your inner being to the best of your ability. (There's no "wrong" way to do this.)

In Chapter Six, we'll explore Barbara Hand Clow's work and her book, *Awakening the Planetary Mind*. Clow examines the overarching psychological patterns in the collective consciousness and subconscious, paying attention to our primal urges so that we can exercise our will to become more radically compassionate— both with ourselves and others—while we continue to transcend the constrictions of the self-imposed cage. We'll also focus on the anterior cingulate cortex (ACC)—the region of the brain that can be our ally in diminishing the strong influences of the limbic system.

SIX

Becoming the Master of
Your Awareness

*

I said to my soul, be still, and wait without hope
For hope would be hope for the wrong thing; wait without
love
For love would be love of the wrong thing; there is yet faith
But the faith and the love and the hope are all in the waiting.
Wait without thought, for you are not ready for thought:
So the darkness shall be the light, and the stillness the danc-
ing

—T. S. Eliot, "The Four Quartets"

We are a wounded species on the verge of recovery, and we
are poised to undertake the brave journey into our brilliance.

—Barbara Hand Clow

My heartbeat raced madly as the hairs on my arms and the back of
my neck stood on end. I was pretty much in all-out panic. It was a
few years ago when I was hiking alone and came face to face with a
big, bad, brown bear. Even though I'd been educated on what action

93

(or non-action) to take, all preparation vanished in the face of this massive, wooly beast.

The bear, on the other hand (thank God), seemed to be having a dupe-de-doo kind of day. When s/he did flash a gaze in my direction, I stood paralyzed, cowering behind a tree. Of course, had s/he decided to become aggressive, that strategy would have provided zero protection.

It turns out I'm not the rugged nature-woman I'd characterized myself to be. Instead, I was just a city girl dressed up in hiking clothes afraid of getting eaten alive (or worse, being badly maimed and left alone to bleed to death).

The big bad bear sauntered off shortly after our meeting, completely unimpressed. S/he went on down her happy trail in search of something more interesting to do than to taunt terrified me. It took the rest of the afternoon for me to breathe normally again.

The alpine area where I live is the brown bear's natural habitat—and was so before any humans set foot here. These bruins roam wide swaths of the territory and will go pretty much anywhere to obtain the ninety pounds of food per day they need to prepare for hibernation. Now habituated to human environments, they occasionally raid garbage cans in town, including my own, as an easy source. Even so, the place that I am most afraid of having another rendezvous (no matter how many times I'm advised to chill) is not my own backyard, but rather the exact spot where I encountered that bear a few years ago—in the deep dark woods.

The memory of that experience made its mark. Every time I now approach that forest, my anxiety about impending danger is exaggerated out of proportion to any real threat. Brown bears aren't aggressive unless you startle them or get in between a mother and her cubs. It's our cuddly-looking polar friends to the north that you have to watch out for. It turns out that hybrid is the only carnivore in the wild that will hunt down humans as prey. But despite this knowledge about brown bears, it's hard for me to follow T. S. Eliot's advice about "being still and waiting without hope" when I remember my encounter with that 800-pound beast.

Anxiety is a uniquely human phenomenon. While associated with fear, it involves the more sophisticated process of anticipation. We are the only species on the planet to project a scenario into the future that's based on past experience—either our own or someone else's. Anxiety is all about what *could* happen, which can fuel overactive imaginations.

From Catastrophism to Universal Human

Barbara Hand Clow, internationally acclaimed researcher and teacher on the development of human consciousness, discussed the scientific theory of "catastrophism" in her book, *Awakening the Planetary Mind*. Using the latest findings of earth science, prehistorians, and archeology, she posited that periodic, instantaneous geological cataclysms occurred in between long periods of slow change, and that these cataclysmic events directly influenced the course of human development. The most recent of these disasters occurred some 11,500 years ago, when the earth was nearly destroyed by floods and earthquakes.

Clow referred to the work of geologist D. S. Allen and science historian J. B. Delair, who believe that a supernova (the explosion of a star) likely shattered near our solar system around the time of the proposed disaster. Allen and Delair have suggested that when fragments of this supernova approached earth, it became a "field of horror," lodging trauma deeply into the collective subconscious, perhaps predisposing our current human propensity to scan for catastrophe. Could this event explain why we as a species are somewhat stuck in the back of our brains (the limbic system)?

Is our current human inclination to be persuaded by pessimism, and turning to dopamine delivery devices for relief, all part of the natural progression from reptile to mammal to us? Or, is it possible that because of a universal traumatic event that occurred when our current brains were developing, our species is often inclined to dip into the below-neutral zone?

The late visionary and futurist Barbara Marx Hubbard identified those of us who are "poised to undertake the brave journey into our brilliance" as "universal humans" or people prepared to "co-create a future equal to our full potential." We can then offer that potential by way of our service to the world, helping to transcend the current challenges on our planet. It's my belief that if we're going to meet that full potential of ours, we're going to have to unlearn some of the stuff that suspends the opportunity.

What do universal humans look like? Are they compassionate, tolerant, and focused on how they can create and expand, rather than dwelling on what they are against or afraid of?

Regardless of why we are the way we are at our current stage of development, can we strengthen the parts of ourselves that will catapult us into "our brilliance?"

T. S. Eliot's "getting still" may just be a technique to help us unwind programming that no longer serves us. That said, our matrix minds seem to want us to do anything but quiet down. What follows in this chapter is more information about why that may be, and how we can expand beyond the limiting conditions that restrict us.

Rites of Passage

I once stumbled across a show on the weather channel entitled "Fat Guys in the Woods." For each episode of the series, survivalist Creek Stevens selected a different trio of overweight, couch-potato-type men with various backgrounds and took them into nature for a week. He taught them survival skills in challenging environments, ranging from desert climates to the mountains. I found myself intrigued while watching these men learn to live as primitive people—catching food with their bare hands, finding water, building shelters, and making fire.

After each show, the men shared their experiences and reflected on how their ordeals of the week transformed them in many ways. "I feel more gratitude and personal worth," one man reported.

"I definitely feel less fear—if I can survive for a week starting out with nothing more than a knife and a liter of water, I feel like I can do anything," another said.

In *The Language of Emotion*, educator Karla McLaren offers interesting insights into how rejecting the traditions, rituals, and coping strategies typically taught in tribal cultures could explain some of our post-modern challenges as a species—such as being overly influenced by the more primitive parts of our brains. McLaren suggests that in the absence of certain experiential activities to train youth for adulthood, like sending them out alone in nature to fend for themselves, contemporary civilizations are skipping a developmental step in the maturation process. By successfully negotiating certain trials in harsh environments (like the fat guys in the woods, only at a younger age), McLaren believes that higher levels of reasoning in the newer parts of our brain would be activated.

In hazardous situations, you have to respond with the appropriate action or suffer the consequences. When you *do* survive the perils of the wild, you emerge with a new awareness. You learn that you can maneuver on your own without anyone else intervening on your behalf, reducing innate fears and perhaps the tendency to watch for the worst-case scenario.

It might be interesting to note, however, that most of the wilderness training in tribal cultures has been for boys. Girls were shown how to tend the fires of the hearth and support the boys/men when they came home from their adventures. Of course, women in post-modern cultures have made impressive advances beyond just tending the fires of the hearth, particularly in the West. We have come of age in various ways, regardless of whether or not we've ever survived a few nights alone in the wilderness.

Even so, I believe there are subliminal messages buried in the collective female psyche that cause us to lean toward dependency and even learned helplessness—regardless of how far up the corporate ladder we crawl. For some of us, that learned helplessness is perpetuated by our environments and our families of origin. If I'm correct, these messages are residue of our ancestry and primal past when we were taught to depend on might and manpower to keep us safe from life-threatening situations.

In most primitive cultures, women weren't shown how to defend themselves. Maybe it's time to mimic the culture in "Avatar," James Cameron's film where both girls and boys are trained how to negotiate their rugged and treacherous terrain (however that terrain might show up in post-modern times).

Daniel Pinchbeck, contemporary journalist and author, agrees with McLaren that going through a rite of passage ordeal activates higher levels of functioning in the prefrontal cortex, which helps mitigate fear-based thinking. He says that unless children going into puberty have an opportunity to learn how to rely on their own wits and wisdom, they may become "kiddults." If we miss the chance to practice outsmarting the wolves and the weather (or whatever is stalking us), our propensity may be to cave in to our weaknesses rather than cultivate our strengths. So, if we've skipped an important developmental step, is it possible to pick it up later in life, like the fat guys in the woods, or even me with my own backwoods vignettes?

Or are there other ways we can learn to expand into higher levels of functioning initiated through rites of passage training early on in life?

Unraveling Patterns: Completing the Missing Step

Let's revisit Abraham Maslow's hierarchy of needs theory. He sequenced these in the following way: physiological—food, shelter, water; security—having the resources to live comfortably and to support basic needs; social—a sense of belonging, love and acceptance; esteem—enjoying feelings of personal worth; and the peak experience or self-actualization, which he described as profound moments of love and happiness.

While developing this hierarchy in the context of the maturation process, was Maslow factoring in the need for rites of passage to mitigate human tendencies of fear, doubt, and negativity? Perhaps. If you know on some level that you're capable of surviving and have activated higher levels of functioning, you naturally cultivate a sense of confidence and self-worth. Building on that sense of security, you move on to love and acceptance. From there, you're positioned to expand into your peak experiences.

We referred earlier to the work of renowned psychiatrist Scott Peck, who believed that once a behavior is habituated and conditioned in childhood (as in learned helplessness, the opposite of actualizing full potential), it's difficult to unlearn that behavior in adulthood. While I have a personal understanding of what Peck is saying due to my own learned helplessness as a child and adolescent, I definitely believe that if you did miss out on determining how to fend for yourself early on, you can learn to do it later—regardless of however subtle or profound your level of dependency might be. In fact, as long as you have a beating heart, I suspect it's never too late.

SELF BELONGING

I've been working on strengthening my own bravado for most of my adult life. In my dedication to that end, I spent a month in an Indian ashram sleeping on a cot and sharing a room with eleven other women—co-participants in a silent, twenty-one day retreat. One day, while slopping soap on myself and my laundry in a cold shower (no hot water or washing machines), I remember thinking that I wanted to do *anything* but dig in the narrow place (precisely what retreats are designed for). Instead, I wondered why I ever thought it was a good idea to go to an ashram. By sticking it out for the duration, I certainly didn't learn how to make fire, stave off wild animals, or suck water out of a leaf. But like our chubby friends in the woods, I did learn what I *didn't* need to survive.

After India, my adult son and I camped in various tricky locations while trekking our way up the Inca trail to Machu Picchu. In ascending many a mountain path alone here in Colorado, I've lived through more than a few thunderstorms and that one brush with a bear. While rearing two young boys as a single mother, I drove a two-and-a-half hour commute (each way) to graduate school once a week for three years. In the course of that time, I held down a job and made it to most of my kids' basketball games and practices. My most recent victory? I'm learning to cherish the spaciousness of living alone while tasting the magic of "sweet freedom." Having opened the door to my self-imposed cage, I can really feel the magic in Michael McDonald's words when he belts out that song from his own soul.

All of this may sound like I'm just listing a string of personal accomplishments that aren't a big deal. But for a kid who missed out on some developmental training myself, I've definitely had some growth spurts as an adult. And every time I experience one of those by facing another fear, I believe I'm carving another notch in my noggin for expansion—evidence that the brain has an inherent ability to rearrange itself or to unlearn something old and learn something new to take its place (neuroplasticity in action).

Letting Go of the Habit of Fear

It's a well-known fact in the psychiatric world that people who are exposed to trauma in the past will often subconsciously repress the memory because it's too painful. Some theorists also believe that repressed memory bands from traumatic events are passed down generationally in ancestral threads, such as those in the lineage of Holocaust survivors. This concept was first brought to a sound, scientific understanding by Sigmund Freud, the psychiatrist who focused much of his work on repressed memories and the subsequent defenses developed to keep them undercover.

Consider your dreams as an example of what's stored in your subconscious psyche. Both Freud and Jung believed dreams to hold important messages, though the information often has to be decoded. Peter Gay, the late professor of history at Yale, said, "The subconscious rather resembles a maximum-security prison holding anti-social inmates languishing for years or recently arrived, inmates harshly treated and heavily guarded, but barely kept under control and forever attempting to escape."

As we've discussed before, the overwhelming majority of emotional and mental activity occurs subconsciously (ninety-five percent per Bruce Lipton). To generate most of the achievements that distinguish us as humans, like initiating oral and written language, thinking, reasoning, and remembering, we rely on the complicated processes of our subconscious minds.

As far as memories are concerned, the unpleasant ones can be lodged under our conscious radar and get stuck there because of a shocking event or a series of repeated traumas. Even while hidden, these memories can cause a disturbance when something in the present triggers a flashback to the past. Once your emotions respond with the corresponding feeling—i.e. anger or fear (fight or flight)—a memo from your subconscious activates your autonomic nervous system (the body-mind connection), which then impacts your heart rate, digestion, and respiration.

The autonomic nervous system is made up of two parts: the sympathetic, which activates fight or flight; and the parasympathetic, which has a more dampening effect. One response is excitatory and the other inhibitory.

The part that's aroused during a trigger is the fight or flight response, which is sometimes appropriate to the situation, but often not—as in the case of my concern that I might encounter another bear. The likelihood of my bumping into a bruin and being subsequently attacked is remote, regardless of how many of those creatures are wandering the back country or how often I hike in that part of the forest. Therefore, what we want to do in order to dampen an unnecessary excitatory response is to bring *awareness* to the situation, so that we can start to reprogram the autonomic nervous system and eventually extinguish the effect of the memory.

Many people suffering from Post-Traumatic Stress Disorder (PTSD) typically cope by dissociating from (blocking out) memories from their past trauma. They make their way to the psychiatric hospital (where, as previously mentioned, I was formerly a practicing clinician) when their acute PTSD episodes become unmanageable. I treated one patient—I'll call her Jennifer, whose neck would literally light up with the actual handprints of her perpetrator during a hyperarousal event or flashback.

Even though Jennifer's hospital stay was only long enough to stabilize her, I was able to follow her in outpatient treatment, where with some support and prompts, she could recall the event that had haunted her subconscious for nearly a decade. In her treatment plan, I included an intervention called systematic desensitization.

In this method, the patient is supported in using some type of relaxation technique while holding the memory of the trauma to the point of tolerance. It took considerable commitment on her part, but after a few months of practice, both at home and in sessions, she was well on her way to neutralizing the trauma. Her formula focused on three primary steps: 1) faith in a higher consciousness to which she credited her recovery, 2) a willingness to be vulnerable by uncovering the source of her trauma and face her fear, and 3) being fully committed to engaging in the process of systematic desensitization.

Again, the mind will repeatedly repress what it believes is too painful to process. In having the fierce discipline to face the subconscious predators in her psyche, Jennifer was eventually able to recognize the truth—that the real perpetrator of her pain had been her own subconscious. With this awareness, she was able to forgive herself and the "villain" who violated her. It took her close to a year to neutralize her fear, but it was well worth the time and effort. Ultimately, she was able to touch the hurting place with love and heal it for good.

The Hero's/Heroine's Journey

Joseph Campbell, celebrated as one of the great mythologists and storytellers of the 20th century, created a framework for the spiritual path that he called the hero's (or heroine's) journey. It goes something like this: The hero, who is always flawed, starts out on their journey filled with hope, perhaps often for the wrong thing, and inspiration. Of course, while on the way, they meet up with a number of challenges— some of them particularly daunting—and may, in the face of those, make poor choices—not unlike what I have done. They go through a dark night of the ego/soul, facing repeated run-ins with their weaknesses. At the pinnacle of their suffering, like Naj, my Iranian mentor, they have a breakthrough. An angelic being descends or their inner wisdom swoops up from inside and offers salvation. Our hero then realizes that they and God are one. They've become *enlightened*. They're now able to repeatedly transcend their flaws and want to be of service to others by sharing what they learned.

Matthew Fox, founder of the ministry school I attended, offers a similar process: the *via positiva* (launching off on the path), *via negativa* (running up against obstacles and having dark nights of the ego/soul), *via creativa* (cracking through the shell of our fears from the dark night and allowing our most creative nature to emerge), and *via transformativa* (once transformed, we want to help others).

Transcending Flaws: Becoming Your Own Hero/Heroine

In his overnight sensation, *Psycho-Cybernetics* (1960), Maxwell Maltz suggested that it takes a *minimum* of twenty-one days to change a habit. His book became a bestseller, and many self-help gurus, including Tony Robbins and Zig Ziglar, adopted the philosophy. The interpretation changed over time, however, from "it takes a minimum of twenty-one days" to "it takes twenty-one days to change a habit." And as it turns out, science has since proven it not to be altogether true.

Findings in a study performed by a research team in London and published in the *European Journal of Social Psychology* show that the norm for changing a habit is actually sixty-six days, and in the study, that number varied widely from eighteen to 254 days, depending on the person and variables involved.

My conclusion? I draw on the wisdom of a revered professor, Ana Perez-Chisti, who once said that it takes discipline, detachment, obedience, and surrender to change—regardless of what else is involved.

The following example is a simple representation of what changing a habit looks like. About a year ago, I went to visit my son and forgot my toothpaste. I noticed he used a brand in a stand-up tube with a flat-bottomed screw-on-lid that I found convenient. Following my trip, I purchased a similar stand-up tube and changed the position of my toothpaste from a drawer to the top of the counter. It took about four months for the new habit to take hold—for me to stop reaching for the drawer and instead reach for the top of the cabinet automatically. It was a simple exercise with no challenging memory to neutralize or bad habit to break, such as smoking. Even so, I was determined, disciplined, obedient to the task, and detached from the results. Since my experiment worked, I have every reason to believe that I now have a new pathway in my head that has memorized something different to do other than open the left-hand drawer in my bathroom when it's time to brush my teeth—another example of neuroplasticity.

When it comes to conditions of behavior that are firmly entrenched, like my patterns in relationships with men, I've found that changing my ways is not as simple as rearranging the toothpaste. I've traced at least part of that destructive pattern all the way back to an encounter with a young man I'll call Keith, who was my first crush in kindergarten. I absolutely believed with all my heart that he was as thrilled at the prospect of a passionate playground rendezvous as I was. After weeks of innocent flirtation as five-year-olds, I asked him to meet me on the playground for a kiss. Rather than respond to my invitation, he sprang to his feet and made a beeline for the teacher, tattling my plan in its entirety. Up until that moment, when I allowed Keith's actions to crush my soul and spirit, I'd been an open-hearted, carefree little kid. That all seemed to change in an instant.

I can remember the moment of perceived rejection as vividly as if it had happened ten minutes ago. It marked the beginning of a lifelong pattern in my relationships with men and my relationships in general, where I let others define not only how I feel, but how I feel about myself. Of course, their behaviors toward me weren't really about me. They were influenced by conditions downloaded from their own families of origin, cultures, societies, and maybe even from the collective post-trauma effects of catastrophism.

In Chapter Three, I mentioned Carol Gilligan's theory that while women thrive on intimacy, men typically define themselves by their achievements rather than their connections and attachments. She said men and women often speak of different truths, with men leaning toward autonomy and separation and women toward connection and intimacy. Of course, at the very core of connection is an open heart. When we do open our hearts, we become vulnerable, expressing the very quality that author Brené Brown has shown to be one of the most valuable of human assets.

So how is it that as women, we can come to see a vulnerable, open heart as an asset rather than a deficit, like Brown encourages? What if, in our wholeheartedness, we're so self-belonged that we're unaffected by how someone responds to our actions—or by how we show love? What if, instead of feeling rejected and misunderstood by Keith's response, I could have let the initial shock ping off of me rather than penetrate so deeply? What if I could have set aside my developing female programming, the force influencing me to let Keith's actions determine my state of delight or devastation, and instead create a little internal celebration? I might have rejoiced in being brave enough to open my heart with no guarantees of what would happen, launching into a courageous rite of passage and initiating myself into the art of self-belonging. That Keith couldn't be vulnerable back didn't have anything to do with me. His heart-brain computer had defaulted to the avoid intimacy program, which he immediately uploaded following my invitation.

As it turned out, I didn't have that little internal celebration until well into the future. This is further proof that when an important developmental step is delayed, it can be initiated later—even much later as in my case. I've finally been able to scrape into the bottom of my emotional sludge and use it as compost to fertilize the ground of my being. In so doing, I'm fortified in turning up the volume on my inner, self-belonging voice to such a degree that the echoes of self-doubt—and even self-loathing, are now nearly inaudible. How have I done it?

When you decide to become a self-belonged soul ... You don't have to wait to be chosen by anyone because you have already chosen yourself.

I finally realized that when you put your ear to the mouthpiece of the fear-based world, it will repeatedly shout scorching memos like, "You will never be good enough. You must be prettier, smarter, and sexier than anyone else if you're ever going to be chosen. Of course, you *have* to be chosen. If you aren't, you won't matter at all."

When you decide to become a self-belonged soul, you'll stop listening to this empty rhetoric. You've learned that the opposite of what the fear-based world wants to teach you is true. You know that you're just fine exactly as you are, regardless of your image in the outside world. You don't have to wait to be chosen by anyone because you've already chosen yourself. You accept your flaws and celebrate your strengths, and you're clear about both. You don't try to fix yourself to match up to anyone else's ideas or expectations about how you ought to be. Instead, you just focus on becoming more fully who you are every time you inhale. You're first a good friend to yourself and then a good friend to others — including your partner. You don't hold back in showing up and putting yourself out there — zits, warts, and all — even if it scares the hell out of you.

You do get scared, really scared, but you go ahead and take action anyway, while giving yourself permission to mess up. When you don't mess up, you celebrate. When you do, you collect yourself, dust off your regret, and try again. You're honest to the core — except when your loving, compassionate discernment advises you not to be. You listen to yourself with your whole heart in the same way you listen to others. You don't try to avoid pain. Instead, you open your heart to it inch by inch, as you let the pain instruct you. You're exceedingly loving and aren't afraid to show it — regardless of how you're perceived — because the loving part of you is the very best part.

Uploading the "Right" Genes: Epigenetics

The newly emerging science of epigenetics, as previously discussed, is the study of variations in the cells, or epigenetic markers atop your DNA, caused by the influence of external events that switch genes off and on. Genes can express themselves either too strongly or too weakly, depending on certain factors like the choice to smoke or not smoke, or to eat too much or not eat too much. In other words, it has now been shown that genes can be uploaded (turned on) or remain dormant, depending on exposure to certain environmental influences.

To make the point, let's use my own family of origin with a history of heart disease as an example. My paternal grandmother, who had a difficult life and was under repeated stress, died of a stroke at seventy years old, while my maternal grandmother, also living under a fair amount of stress, had a fatal heart attack at sixty-three. Neither of the two women made lifestyle choices that would have been considered healthy by today's standards. As far as I know, both ate food saturated in "bad" fat and failed to exercise regularly. One of them smoked. My own parents lived longer, though each had cardiovascular disease resulting in heart attacks. Neither of them exercised regularly, and they both smoked while having relatively unhealthy diets. My brother and I have made different lifestyle choices, and neither of us has signs of heart disease.

As far as other inherited propensities, I have uploaded my share of some, like a family history of anxiety among other mood-related issues. Living under the influence of my Keith experience in kindergarten, a substantial dose of learned helplessness, and watching my mother's reliance on my dad for her sense of well-being and belonging, I had some pretty significant unraveling to do once I became aware of my inclinations.

How much of what we do is caused by bloodlines, environment, development, learned helplessness, karma, the constellation of the stars, or historic calamities? I suspect for most of us, it would take another lifetime or two to calculate it all. What has been helpful for me in my own heroine's journey is to recognize my flaws, learn from my dark nights, and extract wisdom from the scientists and sages. I can use these tools to carve into my consciousness, work on what is malleable, and strengthen the parts that bring balance and meaning to my life. In so doing, I'm a sculptor working from the inside out.

In *How God Changes the Brain*, Newberg (mentioned earlier) points out that empathy, compassion, and social awareness, originating in the anterior cingulate cortex, are newer assets in our human repertoire. The old, reptilian brain had to adapt to incredibly harsh environments and selfishly compete for survival. This more recent part of our anatomy, the ACC or "neurological heart," works to cooperate, rather than resist, while nurturing compassion and acceptance.

According to Newberg, anger, fired from the back of the brain, is the most primal and difficult to control of all the emotions. It interrupts reasoning and causes feelings of righteousness as well as the inability to see the other's view. When anger takes over, not only do we lose the ability to be rational, but we can no longer see that we're acting irrationally. If our anger is met with resistance, the situation usually escalates. When we avoid giving into or reacting to anger and instead step back to take a breath (or step back altogether), we actually increase the blood flow to our frontal lobes and ACC, which helps diminish the activity in our emotional centers. (Recall the parking-ticket vignette discussed in Chapter Three as an example.)

Barbara Marx Hubbard, Lobsang, and Richard Davidson also all agree that cultivating the qualities of equanimity, compassion, gratitude, and joy can aid us in moving beyond the limitations of our subconscious programming. We can then strengthen the regions of the brain designed to negotiate the constant temptation toward the negative. Cultivating compassion, gratitude, and tolerance, starting with ourselves, is the single most important practice to our transformation into universal humans.

Which Wolf Do You Want to Feed?

Well-known Buddhist nun and storyteller Pema Chodron once shared this interesting Native American parable in one of her talks:

> *A grandmother was speaking to her granddaughter about violence and cruelty in the world and how it comes about. She said it was as if two wolves were fighting in her heart. One wolf was vengeful and angry, and the other wolf was understanding and kind. The young woman asked her grandmother which wolf would win the fight in her heart. The grandmother replied, 'The one that wins will be the one I chose to*

feed.'

So how can we train ourselves to feed the right wolf—to have more gratitude, compassion, and tolerance? How can we come to forgive those who we perceive to have let us down, betrayed, or violated us, as my PTSD patient, Jennifer was able to do? Together with Lobsang and Richard Davidson, Andrew Newberg's findings show that spiritual practices strengthen the ACC. Mindfulness meditation or focusing on something in present time like breath, compassion, etc. helps to regulate our reactions over time. It takes determination to change—discipline, detachment, obedience, and surrender. If you've stayed with me this far, I know you have what it takes to feed the right wolf.

* Practice *

Compassion Meditation Revised

For five minutes, practice holding compassion for yourself and your loved ones.

Keep holding compassion for yourself and loved ones while including people that you feel neutral about, like a clerk at the grocery store. Do this for five minutes.

Continue holding compassion for yourself, loved ones, and the people you feel neutral about. Now, include people you resist. Do this for five minutes.

In Chapter Seven, we'll visit a more recent part of our human history dating back to the 1600s, as we consider how the influences of early American settlers—perhaps still under the sway of catastrophism, may have impacted our behavior into the 21st century.

Are both genders predisposed to certain social constructs as a result of belief systems passed along from the early settlers? In addition, we'll continue our discussions of dopamine-driven desire and how this phenomenon can influence behavioral addiction.

SEVEN

Sweet Darkness

*

SWEET DARKNESS

*When your eyes are tired
the world is tired also.*

*When your vision has gone,
no part of the world can find you.*

*Time to go into the dark
where the night has eyes
to recognize its own.*

*There you can be sure
you are not beyond love.*

*The dark will be your home
tonight.*

*The night will give you a horizon
further than you can see.*

*You must learn one thing.
The world was made to be free in.
Give up all the other worlds
except the one to which you belong.*

Sometimes it takes darkness and the sweet

113

confinement of your aloneness
to learn

anything or anyone
that does not bring you alive

is too small for you.

—David Whyte

If "anything or anyone that does not bring you alive is too small for you," you can't blame the person or thing for not bringing you alive. They are just doing what they do. At some point, you may be jolted into realizing that you don't have to stick around for their performance. When you come to such an awareness, you have choices: you can either attempt to negotiate or accept things as they are—fully.

Regardless of what action or non-action you take, the hope is that you'll eventually see that this dark night, when you came to terms with reality, was your launch pad into a world you're meant to be free in—even though the darkness was initially well disguised as a sort of nightmare.

When the shadow that's been hanging over your life morphs into that dark night, you may have reached the edge of your tolerance. Your eyes are tired, and the world seems tired also. You're betwixt and between. You realize you can't stay where you are, but you have no idea how to go forward. It's a dark night, indeed.

What you come to understand is that you have to rely on some measure of faith to access the answers—the same kind of faith that T. S. Eliot said to wait for without hope. For those of us bridled with anxiety, contemplating such a vague devotion can be particularly daunting. In offering your pain to an unfamiliar altar, there's no promise of immediate relief or anything specific at all. Nonetheless, you know what waiting for the wrong thing has cost you. Are you willing to take the risk of choosing the unknown? This dicey option is what trust and surrender are all about.

The Legend of the Hungry Ghosts

Linda Hartoonian Almas, mentioned earlier, suggests that getting a hit of pleasure somewhere in the mix of the unpredictable can keep us coming back for more — if we're hooked on the bait. When we don't get our fix, we may continue to hope for the wrong thing, as in counting on the potential of what *could* show up rather than believing the facts. If this is the case, it's because we trust more in the possibility of something over which we have no control than in our own ability to self-regulate. And self-regulation is the only thing we *do* have the authority to manage.

You may have heard about the legend of hungry ghosts in Chinese Buddhism. These characters are insatiable beings driven by intense emotional needs. Their desires are unquenchable. This unquenchable desire syndrome is what addiction is all about and can show up in a variety of ways. Do you remember our discussion in Chapter Three on dopamine-driven desire and variable rewards? In my case, I'd developed an insidious behavioral addiction to a form of dopamine-driven desire by choosing relationships with men who were both unpredictable and unavailable. The more unavailable and unpredictable they were, the more focused and insatiable I became, determined to fix the situation — until, blind to my own affliction, I let myself become devoured by those hungry ghosts.

In the chapter on love addiction in my first book, *Happily Ever After ... Right Now*, I pointed out that those of us who are afraid of our own power may channel our focus elsewhere as a distraction. Also, if we fear abandonment, we may subconsciously choose a partner who has the same fear. For example, the love addict will go for a guy who may *seem* to be available in the beginning. Except the more she loves, the more he runs. His way of coping with his fear of abandonment is to stay distant and detached. He's just out of reach, semi-available at times (enough to keep her in the game), but never really there for her. Even though this behavior makes him seem cruel, most of it is subconscious. Without realizing it, he's sabotaging his chances for love because he really doesn't believe he deserves it.

When she finally makes her exit, exhausted from repeated frustration, he comes running back. It's then that he demonstrates *his* addictive process, which he's probably not aware of—knowing only that he craves her insatiably now that *she's* not available. His hit of dopamine-driven desire propels him to return to the chase repeatedly.

This cycle of two co-addicted people will cause ongoing despair and desperation for both of them. In my case, I kept trying to fit into all the other worlds of my men rather than giving any time or energy to how I wanted my world to be. Blinded by that unquenchable desire syndrome, I couldn't see that the world was meant to be free in, and that I could give up all of the other worlds by belonging to myself. What follows might offer some clues about how addictive tendencies can carve their way into the psyche and take root in the subconscious.

The Origin of Behavioral Addiction—Dopamine-Driven Desire

According to Gabor Maté in *The Realm of the Hungry Ghosts,* "The possibilities for behavioral addiction are almost infinite." Differing from substance abuse but apparently as persuasive, there are countless scenarios from sex, to gambling, to eating (or not eating), compulsive work, exercise, or a fixation on love that will, according to Maté, "set someone's dopamine circuits into action." The formula for firing up those circuits can look different depending on the individual, but with one common denominator: behavioral addicts have developed a compulsion of looking for the *experience* rather than the substance that they believe will satiate their cravings.

As mentioned in Chapter Three, the compulsions motivated by dopamine-driven desire in our primal beginnings were designed to stimulate curiosity. Endlessly looking for the next reward kept us alive. As we evolved culturally and technologically, however, some of us got stuck in a mire of basic instincts.

As I pointed out in *Happily Ever After ... Right Now:*

> *Becoming attached and eventually addicted to that which you believe is going to make you feel better (save you) is a substitute for soul-growth. And, there are no stand-ins for growing the soul, (which likely will include a few dark nights). So when you attempt to substitute something else for the evolution of your soul, you will probably suffer. The immediate gratification driven by pleasure seeking, which is really the act of avoiding true power and real intimacy, will never bring us the happiness for which we so desperately long. Once we finally begin to realize that we may never attain salvation in the old, familiar way, we will open the portal to end our suffering for good.... Your suffering is a signal for you to make the changes in your operating system that you had previously avoided—hoping for another solution. If you don't heed the warning of that signal and keep repeating the behaviors that have caused you pain, eventually you can spiral into a nightmare of non-stop misery.*

SELF BELONGING

When I wrote those words nearly a decade ago, I believed myself to be on the other side of that spiraling nightmare, having come out of a long-term relationship dynamic some years earlier, similar to the one I played out with Richard. What I've learned is that you can become an intellectual connoisseur on the subject of the "hungry ghost syndrome," but may not fully grasp its meaning until consumed by your own dark night. In the beginning, bottoming out can feel like you're heading directly into a sort of death. Then, over time, the flat-line expands into a boundless horizon, extending your vision to new sunrises and sunsets. One fine day, you realize that you're not beyond love. When you finally give up all of the other worlds and let the night eyes find you — the ones that you have to go inside to see with, you're awakened from that dark night by the internal light of your own belonging.

As we set out on the hero's journey to expand our insights, many of us will be guided to wise teachers who can help jump-start the process. We just have to pay attention to what they say, even though we may initially resist the instruction.

If your attachments or addictions are backing you into a crisis or the risk of repeated self-sabotage, you might decide to put yourself on a self-imposed lockdown like I did. Many a wisdom-keeper before you has done just that. After sitting through a few twilights of their own, just like our Iranian messenger, Naj, did decades ago, they eventually met up with the Indwelling God, who they learned — with considerable practice, would permanently fulfill their deepest needs. Through the benefit of direct experience, they discovered that hunkering down for a few seemingly intolerable dark nights was totally worth the initial inconvenience.

By having the discipline to sit and stew in the compost of your past, you can literally cook yourself into your most creative nature, which is your ticket to transformation. The practice is spiritual, in that it can look and feel like a meditation, but is also an exercise in neuroplasticity in which you carve out new self-regulation circuits in your brain.

If you missed the important developmental step of strengthening your capacity to self-regulate and keep scanning for the dopamine hit to soothe you, you can pick that step up later like the "fat guys in the woods." As your personal research project, I've put some serious effort into cultivating my own self-regulation circuits and find that doing so has definitely brought more lasting rewards than the temporary satisfaction of dopamine-driven desire. When you focus on whatever serves your highest potential and enforce your will and determination to support you, you're destined to experience measurable results and rewards. Maps of my own process, along with more proof of neuroplasticity, will surface as our journey continues.

When you focus on whatever serves your highest potential and enforce your will and determination to support you, you're destined to experience measurable results and rewards.

What Causes What?

Maté offered an explanation for some of the root causes of addiction with the work of D. W. Winnicott, a British pediatrician and psychiatrist. (Winnicott used Maté as one of his prime examples—his drug of choice being work.) Emotional development can be affected by a condition Winnicott described as "proximate separation," which can occur when a parent is unable to tune into her child's needs. Maté's mother had been depressed during his developmental years when her husband was imprisoned at Auschwitz. She admitted to being frequently unavailable to provide adequate child care. Such a predicament may result in a child developing unhealthy coping strategies. Even though proximate separation can be a setup for self-soothing or inadequate self-regulation, it's not about the parent's lack of love or commitment. Instead, it's about how the child perceives they are seen or understood on an emotional level.

Nevertheless, the findings on attunement or proximate separation, however valid, can feel vague and inconclusive. Isn't it possible that none of us are cut out to be completely present and emotionally available for our kids? My own mothering can serve as an example. I can cite instances when I wasn't emotionally present for my developing infant sons. That I loved them way beyond what I could possibly describe here is without question. But I probably had a mild case of postpartum depression following the birth of my first son. After my second was born, I felt pretty overwhelmed and under-supported by their father. Even so, despite any of my failings (or their dad's), these young men have greatly exceeded all of my expectations in remarkable ways.

In the psychiatric world, one of my specialties was working with youth—some in foster care or group homes. A few children had extraordinary resiliency despite their troubled backgrounds, while others fell into predictable patterns of pathology and addiction. I also saw kids from what would appear to be "normal" family environments who had issues with addiction. They seemed to have loving, attentive parents who wanted nothing but the best for them. Others, who had similarly supportive homes, developed eating disorders, a severe form of behavioral addiction, feeling the only way to have control over their lives was to enforce a rigid regimen over what went in (or out) of their bodies.

Were the parents of substance abusers or the eating disordered attuned to them in infancy? Did these kids experience proximate separation issues? How could we in the psychiatric world investigate the true facts of an adolescent's background? We were invariably given highly subjective and possibly biased data, mostly delivered by parents or guardians.

Even though there are categories and criteria for diagnosing presenting issues that help us make an appropriate assessment, all we can do much of the time is speculate as to what caused a certain condition to develop. Nonetheless, in creating a workable treatment plan, it can help to have theories and clues about possible causes.

Meanwhile, the diagnostic and statistical manual of mental illness has expanded from the DSMIV (1994) (Diagnostic and Statistical Manual of Mental Disorders 4th Edition) to an updated version, the DSMV (2016). Either psychopathology in humans has become increasingly complex, or we've gotten more sophisticated in our descriptions of these pathologies. I believe both scenarios are true. Regardless of whatever may be causing our missteps in overcoming our human challenges, we can either see things as discouraging or continue to meet the challenge by altering our course. As a wise mentor once told me, "In healing the soul of humanity, if everyone just did their part, the world would change in an instant—*an instant*."

What if each and every one of us did our part by addressing whatever may be aberrant in our own psyche and inner wiring? If our parents weren't available or present for us, how can we learn how to be available and present for ourselves? Naj can serve as a perfect example of someone who has learned to self-regulate even though he missed out on that developmental step early on. We don't know much about his early childhood, but his experience of being completely cut off from his parents or any nurturing adult at age seven could have been enough to disturb the important developmental stage from seven to fourteen. Yet, I have rarely met a more loving, caring, well-adjusted man. I can only attribute the manifestation of these admirable qualities to his own uncanny way, at age seven, of learning how to cultivate awareness and presence within himself.

As for my own childhood, I believe that both my parents were loving and attentive when my older brother and I were young children. As we matured, things started to change. Our father's temperament became increasingly more unpredictable. He could fly into a rage without warning. Regardless of my mother's attempts at being a good wife by setting aside her talents as a gifted musician, he repeatedly berated her behind closed doors.

My brother overcame the effects of our father's abuse by focusing on self-empowerment. He launched his entrepreneurial spirit early in life and eventually rolled all of his enterprises into a mega-prosperous business, which he sold for a large profit when he'd barely reached middle age. He and his wife relished some wonderful years of retirement until her death from cancer eighteen years later. Not long after her passing, he married another wonderful woman, who'd suffered a loss similar to his, and the two are enjoying life together.

I, on the other hand, grew up on stories of make believe about Prince Charming. Instead of following my brother's example by empowering myself, I escaped into the fairy tale fantasies for answers as to how to feel better. In adolescence, I developed a pattern of under-performing in school, focusing instead on how to be chosen by boys. My deepest driving desire, which wasn't necessarily lined up to my "dharma code" (my life purpose), was to be married and have kids. Unlike my brother, who concentrated on how he could save himself, I kept looking for someone else to do it for me. Of course, it took a colossal tumble down the rabbit hole of my fantasies to jolt me out of that illusion.

Did I develop proximate separation at some point? Was I somehow conditioned to self-soothe instead of self-regulate? Did I take on some of my mother's propensities to focus on my man and how to please him? Did I choose men whose personality profiles and appearance resembled my father's?

Nancy Friday wrote a book in the 1970s called *My Mother/Myself,* which I read in my twenties. Friday's message was this: "If women are to be able to love without possessing, to find work that fulfills them, and to discover their full sexuality, they must first acknowledge their identity as separate from their mothers."

As I have repeatedly suggested, perhaps the single most important element in untangling the complexities of our patterns is to become *aware* of our propensities—both the ones that serve us and those that don't. In my case, I wanted to belong to each man I've loved (too much) before I learned how to love and belong to myself—just like my mother did—and perhaps as many others before her had done in the course of our ancestral journey.

Colette Dowling, who wrote *The Cinderella Complex,* joins Robin Norwood, Judith Viorst, and Carol Gilligan as a 1980s torchbearer by being among the first to encourage women to wake up and become aware of how they operate in relationships. Dowling described the "good woman syndrome," which defines how women like my mother and myself lose our identity to the men we become attached to. The *Cinderella Complex* refers to a woman's fear of independence rooted in a desire to be taken care of. "She does her damnedest to please others ... these women have an acute lack of meaning in their lives ... their only sense of competency is to get what they want through dependency." Of course, in always seeking to please others, we repeatedly lie to ourselves.

The Career Front for the Twenty-First Century Woman

Even though it's been about thirty-five years since those 1980s torchbearers came forward, I haven't seen dramatic changes in how some women (if not many) operate in their relationships. Nonetheless, statistics show that we've made great strides on the career front. For example, women outnumber men in the recent graduating classes of several top-ranking institutions. NYU Law's 2017 class was fifty-five percent female; Berkeley School of Law's 2020 class was sixty-five percent female; and Yale Law School's 2020 class was fifty-three percent female. In 2017, one year after women first nudged past men in law-school enrollment, they made the same historic leap in medical school: at 50.7 percent, more women than men are now on the academic path to become doctors.

In 2016, though, female doctors earned 26.5 percent less than men. In 2017, that figure grew, to 27.7 percent. For doctors and lawyers alike the pay chasm persists (or has widened) even though the education gap has closed. The academic achievements of women in each discipline — which for now are undercut by a lack of concomitant earning power — parallel each other in more ways than one. Both law and medical school offer a path to prestigious employment; both law and medicine have been male-dominated fields; and female students at both types of schools have, historically, gone on to earn and achieve less than their male peers.

In general, across all professions, research by PayScale.com shows that the uncontrolled gender pay gap, comparing the ratio of median earnings of women to men, has decreased by only $0.07 since 2015. In 2020, women made only $0.81 for every dollar a man makes.

Creating A Village for Our Kids

Studies performed by the Pew Research Center, which follows social and demographic trends, showed in 2018 that the share of children who will experience life with an unmarried parent is considerably higher than in the past, due largely to the rising fluidity of US families. One estimate suggests that by the time they turn nine, more than twenty percent of US children born to a married couple, and over fifty percent of those born to a cohabiting couple, will have experienced the breakup of their parents. The declining stability of families is linked both to increases in cohabiting relationships, which tend to be less long-lasting than marriages, as well as long-term increases in divorce. Indeed, just over half of solo parents in 2017 had been married at one time, and the same is true for about one-third of cohabiting parents.

As is evidenced throughout this material, I'm a strong advocate for women reaching their full potential (alongside men doing the same), and despite the sobering statistics about pay-scale inequality, studies show that women are certainly capable of establishing equal footing with their male colleagues. All of that said, in today's world, it is likely that in households with children, both parents — plus the overwhelming majority of single parents — will be working outside the home, whether out of need or personal fulfillment. With this being the case, have we in our western culture come up with adequate ways to be fully available for our kids when it's impossible for us to be close to home all of the time?

In Indigenous cultures, the elders are involved in child-rearing, but in post-modern America, families are scattered over wide swaths of the country or the globe, making it difficult for extended families to stay connected. When both parents or the custodial parent work outside the home, and their children are left in daycare or with a sitter for extended periods, isn't it inevitable that these kids will miss out, at least on some level? In most cases, can there really be a substitute for parents or family? One hundred percent of the adolescents I saw in the psychiatric world came from backgrounds involving either parental stress, lack of appropriate supervision, neglect, abuse, or some combination of all of these.

One of my friends and her husband work full time, each maintaining two jobs. Nonetheless, they have never had child care for their now nineteen-year-old daughter. They were both able to shift their schedules so that one of them could be available for her at all times. When such an arrangement isn't possible, how can we create a village of support for our children? What will it take for us to make this a priority?

Sin by Silence

Then, there's domestic violence, which is hardly a new phenomenon. Even so, it wasn't until the late 1970s that our country began to recognize the behavior as criminal, prosecuting those (primarily men) responsible and developing hotlines and safe houses for victims (primarily women and children). Today, forty years after my own childhood experiences with domestic violence, it remains a tragic threat to women and families at all levels of American society, not to mention what's happening in the rest of the world. I was shocked to see an ad in the paper recently in my safe little high Alpine village, for a women's self-defense class at a local gym. It read: "A woman is beaten every nine seconds in the United States," a fact confirmed by the Women's Resource Center to End Domestic Violence.

A 2020 study released by the University of Louisville notes that family and domestic violence (including child abuse, intimate partner abuse, and elder abuse) is a common problem in the United States. Family and domestic violence are estimated to affect ten million people in the United States every year. It is a national public health problem, and virtually all healthcare professionals will at some point evaluate or treat a patient who is a victim of some form of domestic or family violence. Unfortunately, each form of family violence begets interrelated forms of violence, and the cycle of abuse (repeated acts of violence in a cyclical pattern) is often continued by exposed children into their adult relationships, and finally to the care of the elderly. Domestic and family violence includes a range of abuse including economic, physical, sexual, emotional, and psychological toward children, adults, and elders.

Is violence and rage a form of behavioral addiction? Do violent men, often seemingly loving in the beginning of a relationship, actually fear intimacy, thereby repeatedly sabotaging their chances for love inside a Dr. Jekyll/Mr. Hyde approach to life? Are they somehow hungry ghosts in this behavioral cycle?

Sin By Silence, a 2009 award-winning documentary filmed behind prison walls, tracks the lives of women who have killed their abusers. Together, they tell stories about cycles of terror and hope, while advocating for a future free from domestic violence.

Gloria Steinem, leader in the feminist movement, once suggested in an interview that crimes of domestic violence are actually acts of supremacy, offering no positive outcomes for those who commit them other than a brief period of exercising control over someone else. Is this behavior influenced by dopamine and the cognitive quirk the chemical creates? Can you see how the cycle of violence could follow the pattern of intermittent reward with addictive components as discussed in Chapter Three?

The Love Resistant — Profiles of Abusers

After watching *Steve Jobs*, the 2015 film starring Michael Fassbender about the late Apple computer guru, I did some research, discovering that some of the script was fictional. Even so, from what I could gather, the underlying themes about his unpredictable fits of rage, callous character, and challenges with intimacy were at least partially accurate. Jobs, who died of cancer in October 2011, was adopted as an infant. Apparently, just a month following placement with a family, he was returned to the agency. Not long after his first adoption failed, young Steve was brought under the care of Paul and Clara Jobs, who wanted to adopt him but didn't meet the criteria set by his biological mother, Joanne Schieble.

Apparently, Schieble stipulated that any prospective parents had to be college-educated, so for close to a year, the Jobs couple didn't know if they would be able to keep baby Steve. In the movie, Steve Jobs says that since Clara was unsure if she'd ever be his adoptive mother, she kept her distance and didn't bond with him until the adoption was final. If this is true, did her lack of full connection with him cause proximate separation and subsequent challenges in his interpersonal relationships, including anger management and control issues?

My own father was born in 1916 in the middle of World War I (1914-1918) to Nora Belle Hull when she was just sixteen years old. Married to George Arthur Hull, four years her senior, both were formally educated only through the fifth grade. George supported the family as a mechanic and tool-maker. During Dad's developmental years, Nora took in laundry to help with expenses. In preparation for the task, she pumped water from an outdoor well, which she boiled in batches on a wood stove.

My dad slept on a cot in the kitchen and worked at various jobs to help the family survive the Great Depression. He managed to secure a loan for college and worked his way through law school, finishing before he was drafted in World War II, in which he played a notable role. Putting himself at considerable risk, he attended secret meetings in order to prepare President Roosevelt's map room to show the location of troops. Dad revealed that at one point it was feared Hitler's German army was close to winning the war.

Did my father's challenges growing up and the stressful circumstances to which he was exposed during the war contribute to challenges with his interpersonal relationships, anger management, and occasional all-out rage?

Richard's father was also a World War II veteran. He remained in

Germany after the war and sent for his wife and Richard when he was a few months old. Once together in Germany, the trio remained until Richard was a toddler, after which they returned to the US. The family grew to a group of seven, and during Richard's early adolescence, they struggled to stay together due to financial challenges.

During my relationship with Richard, he frequently discussed how he was affected by his family's hardships. Did those difficulties influence how he operated when we were together? Did my childhood circumstances have an effect on how I behaved with Richard?

Are We Still Influenced By the Puritan Ethic?

Besides our own immediate childhoods, are there historical influences that might play a part in how we function in relationships and in general? Consider the 1692 witch trials of Salem, Massachusetts, which is likely the worst misogynistic massacre in American history, for example. Twenty people, mostly women, were murdered and up to 150 imprisoned. Those targeted had become the projection of public mass hysteria.

The Puritans who settled in Salem, survived the near intolerable ravages of the sea, putting them at risk of hopelessness by the time they finally docked on American shores. Having finally landed, they found themselves literally on the edge of civilization. From the beginning of their escapade, they were riddled with anxious anticipation and lived in a constant state of fear, not knowing what to expect in their new homeland. They were either repeatedly looking over their shoulder to protect themselves from the "savages," whose land they now shared, or worried about sheer exposure to what seemed to be insurmountable challenges posed by the elements and their new neighbors.

Apparently, there was also a third, less tangible fear—the fear of Satan and how his havoc might manifest among them. The ones considered most suspect were women outliers or those not living in accordance with the strict religious standards of the day. They were often seen as rebels and renegades. Even so, perhaps all Puritans could be seen as rebels and renegades, having come to the new land mostly to break away from the religious standards of England. At the time, women were also regarded as the "weaker sex" and more susceptible to lust and sin, a belief that could perhaps be traced to the story of Adam and Eve. Especially questionable were women who were more free-spirited and exploring their own spiritual practices, perceived by some as witchcraft. The people most likely to question or persecute them feared what would result if these outspoken, independent women influenced others.

In gathering some of the information about the Salem witch trials, I discovered my own "witch" relative. Her name was Elizabeth Bates, a woman said to be a spiritualist who could supposedly levitate tables and heal with her hands. By all accounts, she was considered an outlier instead of a shape-shifter. The witch trials had taken place just a mere 145 years before Elizabeth's birth in 1837 and only 268 years before my own. Have the threads of belief systems and the judgments behind them found their way into my ancestry and possibly many other lineages alongside my own?

I can only imagine what it must have been like to live in Elizabeth's skin, particularly in light of the rigid opinions held by the Protestant, patriarchal Hull lineage, which perhaps dates all the way back to the trials in Salem. Nonetheless, all things considered, if you will, join me in taking a moment or two to consider the course your own consciousness might have taken under similar circumstances as what the Puritans endured in the 1600s. Perhaps putting ourselves in their shoes and in the shoes of others in our own time will help us to have more understanding and tolerance.

As for my father, Steve Jobs, and Richard, the three men whose brief profiles I have highlighted here, statistics prove that there are many others who share personality profiles similar to theirs. Is it too much of a generalization to assume that they at least, in part, inherited some of their tendencies from ancestors—possibly dating back to the early days of American civilization or before?

Here is what I wrote in *Happily Ever After ... Right Now* about men with similar profiles:

> *I have watched them do whatever they do to avoid feeling what they feel, and when they can stand it no more—retreat into their caverns of silence. Only those caves are never silent for them. They are crammed in every corner and crevice with the voices of failure and fear that continue to haunt and torture them. I have lived with and loved these cave-dweller men until I thought my guts would fall out. I have watched them occasionally dabble in their vulnerability long enough to be tender and gentle, only to return to their stony, stoic silence. And when they haven't known what to do with the emotion and judgment that continues to bounce off the walls of their skulls—they may lash out and rage their feelings at others—including me.*

Good Lord, what suffering have they endured? Can we have compassion for them, considering what they've been through? What is it like to be under pressure to perform and be potent at every level? Haven't they been bullied into believing they've got to bring home the biggest slab of bacon in order to even matter?

Of course, what I've finally had to face is the fact that there's nothing I can do to save these men from whatever is going on inside them that causes their misery—which may translate into projecting their suffering onto me in one form or another. All I can do is recognize what's happening, return to what stabilizes me— self-belong and get the hell out of the way—quite possibly for good.

I admit to many times when I most certainly felt like a victim. In doing a rewind of the Richard reel, I can see in living color how patterns and bloodlines played an important role in how things unfolded between us. Also, if karma is factored into the mix, who knows what I was attempting to resolve from other lifetimes with this man and others.

I'm comforted by the *Bhagavad Gita* Hindu scripture: "Even he with the worst karma who ceaselessly meditates on Me (the Indwelling God) quickly loses the effects of his past bad actions. Becoming a high-souled being, he soon attains perennial peace. Know this for certain. The devotee who puts his trust in Me never perishes."

The Influence of Women's Subjugation

One of the first statements challenging the political and social repression of American women was written in 1848, just eleven years after the birth of my ancestor, Elizabeth Bates. Called the Declaration of Sentiments and modeled after the Declaration of Independence, five women came together to write it, listing legal grievances and the limited educational opportunities for women. It was written in Seneca Falls, New York, in the middle of the Iroquois Confederacy, by women who were well aware of rights that the indigenous women among them enjoyed but which they were denied. In the Iroquois model, the presence of both women's and men's councils honored feminine and masculine principles equally.

In contrast, women in most cultures in the 19th century were considered the property of their husbands. The men held complete authority over their wives, including the right to discipline them through measures of their own choosing. Since women were considered incompetent in the mid-1840s, they couldn't vote or testify in court. All legal movements that led to democracy, which began in Greece and eventuated in the Declaration of Independence in the United States, excluded women.

The 19th Amendment to the Constitution giving women the right to vote was introduced in Congress forty-five times before it was ratified in 1920. A few years following that milestone, the feminine voice hit a sort of lull until World War II in 1939, when women were expected to fill the void in the workplace left by men going overseas. Out of necessity, women showed up and rose to the occasion, demonstrating that they were not only competent, but could manage independently without a man to lean on. After the war ended in 1945, women returned to domestic roles, tending the household and taking care of kids. Those who remained in the workforce were mostly single and did so because they had no alternative.

I was influenced by the post-war stereotype. Under my mother's tutelage, I learned the art of homemaking in preparation for marriage and family. I was fortunate to have an undergraduate education by the time I was married, but I wouldn't put it to use until years later.

Even when I first heard Gloria Steinem speak in 1971 at Wichita State University to a capacity crowd in the basketball stadium, I was only mildly curious about her message and really just followed the momentum to her event. While some of her ideas resonated—principally that most jobs aside from prostitution didn't require a penis or vagina—I wasn't inclined to burn my bra or march in a Women's Liberation parade. Most of what she said was completely new to me—that women had just as much to offer as men in terms of their careers and social contributions. At that time, it was more comfortable for me to stay in the enchanted myths of 1960s Americana, while focusing on my looks and finding my version of Prince Charming.

By the time I enjoyed my right to vote at age twenty-one—the year I heard Steinem speak, women had only been permitted the privilege of participating in the political process for fifty-one years. Steinem was speaking on the shoulders of women who fought for our rights, including that circle of five in Seneca Falls.

The first two phases of women claiming their power, launched at the end of the Industrial Revolution and extending into the mid-twentieth century, started with political energy fueled by small groups. The third phase, building on the first two, seems to be happening in our hearts, souls, and psyches, which I've had the privilege of observing and being a part of since the 1970s. From that time forward, I've watched women's groups morph into an enormous swell of spirituality, manifesting in a variety of ways—including the expansion of the #metoo movement toward the end of 2017, which galvanized the efforts of those coming forward with sexual abuse allegations. It began in Hollywood with the citing of Harvey Weinstein as an offender, and then included other celebrities like Louis C.K., Charlie Rose, and Matt Lauer, to name a few.

When Googling the key words "women's spiritual groups" just now, the results showed 24,600,000 possibilities with pages and pages to choose from. Isn't it possible that these groups can be organic containers for stimulating conscious awareness? Isn't it also possible that spiritual groups could be the vehicles that catapult us into a new phase of our evolutionary status, where we come together to support our individual and collective truths by staring down both our inner and outer predators? Is this the time in human history when we as women will finally be claiming our power instead of denying it? Do we dare? And can self-belonging help us make that leap?

Amping Up Your Self-Regulation Circuits

As you know by now, the process of self-belonging is ultimately about how to strengthen your connection to the Indwelling God—transcending anything that gets in the way, from your childhood experiences to influences in your personal or collective historical past.

In order for me to do so, I've had to sit in the sweet confinement of my aloneness, staying put until I could feel my feet growing roots. Prior to making that commitment to dig into that narrow place, my recidivism (relapse) was predictable, as evidenced by the many times I let my dopamine-driven desire persuade me to return to Richard. In the beginning of my recovery, I dealt with intense, unrelenting cravings. My biology was on fire, screaming for a fix. I had to relentlessly exercise my will in order to avoid acting on those cravings until they eventually diminished and finally dissolved.

The process of sitting in your aloneness is what self-regulation is all about. It's determining how you can be present and available for *you*—even when you don't believe anyone else is there for you or was there for you in the past. Your longing is nothing more than the desire for connection, and the only way you can truly be intimate with another is to connect more deeply with yourself.

The process of self-belonging is ultimately about how to strengthen your connection to the Indwelling God—transcending anything that gets in the way.

So how on earth do you do this? One sure way, which I know by heart, is to dig down into that narrow space at the precise moment when you feel that gap between you and Source starting to widen. This usually happens when you find yourself craving someone else. It's precisely when your tender heart is the most raw and vulnerable that you're the most available to receive the Indwelling God's healing influence. Who or what else could possibly fulfill your deepest need but Her? She's there, patiently waiting to escort you to your inner paradise.

It has been over six years since I launched the healing journey that supported me in letting go of my unhealthy attachment to Richard. While in the process, I've watched new feelings, habits, desires, and lack of desires alter the landscape of my expedition. My latest discovery is a blossoming love for my life as a single woman. To my surprise, I love hitting the floor in the morning, sliding into my fuzzy slippers, and igniting my little espresso machine to make a brew for one. I love charting the course of my day, as I consider what action or non-action will light up the next fourteen hours. Writing a blog about my latest inspiration? Meditating? Journaling? Going to the coffee shop and having someone else make me an Americano? Most importantly, my list of cravings has diminished under the influence of a dedicated focus to healing and wholeness.

It's so simple. If I'm attached to a person, place, thing, or to results of any kind, I'm not free. If, on the other hand, I've disciplined myself to be detached from every outcome—asking for guidance from the Indwelling God, following that dutifully, and surrendering all to the Divine—I'm completely free. Janis Joplin belts out her version of freedom in her classic hit, "Me and Bobby McGee." Be sure to give it a listen when you get a chance—that song carries a powerful message about freedom.

Yes, the world was made to be free in. With the help of the Indwelling God, I've brought myself alive and into my creative nature, as evidenced by my passion to write this book, systematically putting the words on paper, and finding ways to make it all available to you. You, too, can seize the opportunity to be free, and when you do, "the night will give you a horizon further than you can see."

My dear fellow self-belonging enthusiasts, from my own experience—still in progress, meditating on God is *precisely* what will permanently fulfill your deepest need, and ultimately resolve all of your human traumas and debacles. This includes the realization of whatever and whomever is too small for you because they don't bring you alive.

In the chapters that follow, beginning with Chapter Eight, devoted to the topic of forgiveness, I'll delve deeper into my commitment to self-belonging—to diminishing my inner fears, dissolving everything hard, violent, horrific, or obsessed. In continuing to build, strengthen, and nurture the Indwelling God, I'll fortify both the Divine Masculine and Divine Feminine as the primary influences in my life.

* Practice *

For the next few days, when your feet hit the floor in the morning, contemplate these questions: *What brings me alive? What makes me happy? What are my strengths? What do I want to contribute? How do I want to be remembered?*

EIGHT

Sweet Freedom

*

Our truest deepest self is completely free. It is not crippled or compromised by past actions or concerned with identity or status. It comprehends that it has no need to fear the earthly world and therefore it has no need to build itself up through fame or wealth or conquest. This is the true spiritual self. How do we get closer to it? We must use everything in our power to cultivate and bring it to light. And we do this by manifesting love and compassion. They make up the very fabric of the spiritual realm.

— Eben Alexander

Patriarchal authority is the unwritten code that has allowed a few — usually men, even in post-modern times, to have dominance and power over the many. This code has repeatedly persuaded humanity toward an imbalance of power, creating division and separatism while upholding a hierarchical approach to our social structure. This control is asserted through a variety of ways, all of which can be used to manipulate outcomes for personal or collective gain.

Given what we've been learning about the persuasive influence of dopamine, is it possible that this neurotransmitter could be a factor in affecting the behavior of people in positions of power?

Some theorists speculate that during the Paleolithic era, preceding

3000 BCE, society was female-centric. Since women possessed mysterious life-giving powers before men's role in conception was understood, they were held in high regard. Women were gatherers, harvesting food and carrying water to their communities. Men were trained to hunt, but neither task was seen as more valuable than the other. A natural interdependency created a society where people were linked rather than ranked. Those who subscribe to this theory believe that the homeostasis of this peaceful time shifted because of a cataclysmic event, as we discussed in Chapter Six. During and after that event, the testosterone-driven qualities of aggression and competition became more prominent and valued—the mindset at the core of a patriarchal culture.

If there was a cataclysm that changed the course of history and predisposed us to scan for the catastrophe, is it possible that the nature of crisis made men appear more capable of handling calamity purely by virtue of their stamina and physical prowess? If so, did their primal tendencies to react with aggression and competition unseat women's status from that point forward? Have we as a collective bought into the idea of survival through force?

Regardless of how the current patriarchal paradigm evolved, or whether you believe there is such a paradigm, the global unrest that surrounds us today is palpable, as force and aggression thrive. It happens right here on our own shores through extremist organizations and terrorist cells like the Ku Klux Klan—the oldest American hate group, which has been promoting white supremacy and various crimes against Blacks since 1865; the New Black Panther Party, members of which were said to have carried guns into the Republican Convention in 2016 to intimidate participants; and Antifa, an anti-fascist left-wing group that employs sporadic violence and divisionary tactics to influence the US electorate. Our current global landscape is also disrupted by assaults related to gang violence, drug and human trafficking, mass shootings, domestic violence, and various other forms of brutality.

Since the 911 attacks on the World Trade Center by Al-Qaeda, this Islamic terrorist group or its factions have continued to stage subsequent assaults in locations across the world. The Taliban, an Islamic fundamentalist political movement waging war against women's education, attempted to murder eleven-year-old Malala Yousafzai in October 2012 because she advocated schooling for girls in Pakistan.

According to the US State Department, 800,000 people are trafficked across international borders every year—eighty percent of whom are female and half are children. These people are sold, kidnapped, or promised a brighter future only to be caught in the net of the sexual slave trade or forced labor. Human trafficking is a thirty-two billion dollar a year industry—seven billion more than McDonald's makes in a year. Of course, these examples are among the very worst versions of attempted control by patriarchal authority.

When using Abraham Maslow's scale as a way to measure where we humans currently are as a collective, it would appear that we may be, at least in part, stuck in the fundamental phases of survival. Remember that the first on the list of his hierarchy of needs model has to do with the basics—acquiring shelter, food, and security. Once these are obtained, Maslow says we can move to mastering love and a sense of belonging (starting with ourselves), together with respect and esteem. When we master how to acquire food and shelter and learn how to love both others and ourselves, we have built a foundation for the full-on-expression of our gifts, or what he called self-actualization.

Given the current social statistics regarding world distribution of wealth, it's understandable that we as a species might be stuck in survival.

According to Anthony F. Sharrocks, former director of the World Institute for Development Economics Research, the richest ten percent of adults in the world own eighty-five percent of global household wealth, while the bottom half collectively owns barely one percent. Even more strikingly, the average person in the top ten percent owns nearly three thousand times the wealth of the average person in the bottom ten percent. These are some of the results that have emerged from a study of the distribution of household wealth undertaken for the UNUWIDER project on personal assets from a global perspective.

Finding Our Way to the Light

Amidst all the chaos, is it possible to create a sweeping shift in consciousness? Can we harness the forces of good to eclipse the evil? Is there hope that we as a species can find our way out of the survival phases of our development and move our way up Maslow's scale toward our full potential?

Biologist, author, and philosopher Rupert Sheldrake has created breakthrough theories on a phenomenon he calls "morphic resonance." Building on Carl Jung's concept of the "collective subconscious," Sheldrake hypothesizes that every species carries a collective memory of how to operate, which can be altered when a certain percentage of that species collaborates on changing their story. His theory suggests that there are "mysterious telepathy-type interconnections between organisms and of collective memories within the species." Sheldrake believes that information is transferred either consciously or subconsciously, by communication through an invisible energy grid, which he describes as the morphogenetic field.

In physics, critical mass is the turning point that generates a sustained chain reaction. Is it possible that Sheldrake is right? When a sufficient number of individuals agree on change, the combined energy of merging atoms, subatomic particles, protons, and quarks—

making up an invisible energy grid, may come together to create a sustained chain reaction of collective thought—rearranging or perhaps replacing previous agreements.

Jung believed that every individual consciousness is significantly swayed by "unavoidable influences exerted upon it by its environment … [among which is] a second psychic system of a collective, universal, and impersonal nature identical in all individuals." Between 1929 and 1939, Jung wrote extensively on these influences and believed that the human archetype (a pattern that's repeatedly replicated) could be changed by that second psychic system, although he couldn't explain how the process worked.

Sheldrake offers that such an explanation can be found in morphic resonance, or the unspoken agreements and memory transferred among organisms of the same species. He says, "A group's thoughts, actions, and insights create an energy pattern (resonance), which makes it more likely that people otherwise unaware of the thoughts or occurrences, will experience similar insights, etc." Mainstream scientists, who continue to buy into the more mechanistic view of how things work, using theories asserted by Sir Francis Bacon, Rene Descartes, and Sir Isaac Newton in the 16th and 17th centuries, continue to question Sheldrake's theory. In the mechanistic model, the world is regarded more like a machine rather than a soulful, living organism.

As Sheldrake suggests, suppose we have ways of subconsciously transferring certain unspoken agreements through energy patterns (resonance). When new information influences a few people, causing a change in their beliefs, and others begin to catch on and agree, the new thoughts and ideas build momentum. Once the new energy pattern reaches a certain crescendo, a shift in consciousness occurs. Is this process of morphic resonance one possible explanation for how evolution unfolds?

SWEET FREEDOM

Thom Hartmann, author and former psychotherapist, says:

The dominant (human) story can and does get changed. And, when cultural stories begin to shift, those transporting the new stories are considered oddballs, cranks, or cultists.... Washington and Jefferson were referred to in the British press and among large parts of the American population prior to the Revolutionary War, as misfits and malcontents. But stories change when a certain critical mass is achieved.

Internationally known Jungian analyst, Jean Shinoda Bolen, says in her book, *Goddesses in Older Women*, that people coming together in spiritual circles with a focus on consciousness, which she sees as absent from politics and governance, can have an effect on the human species as a whole. A supporter of Rupert Sheldrake's work and his theory of morphic resonance, she believes that such groups can serve as vessels for creating momentum for a human upgrade.

I once took a course on leadership with revered professor Margaret Wheatley, who offered a challenging directive to those of us that wanted to do our part in changing the human story: she told us to have as many conversations as possible about what mattered to us. Isn't it possible that Jefferson, Washington, and Malala were/are doing just that? What do you suppose Abraham Lincoln was talking about while campaigning for the Emancipation Proclamation that freed the slaves? To change the current narratives, like they all were able to do, we too, must be visionaries, crusaders, and thought leaders—having as many conversations as we can about what matters to us.

Susan B. Anthony of the Women's Suffrage movement collected more than 400,000 signatures in support of the abolition of slavery and founded an organization that campaigned for the rights of both women and African Americans. The "Anthony Amendment," which she presented to Congress, became the 19th Amendment to the constitution in 1920, fourteen years after her death in 1906. Arrested and convicted for voting in her hometown, can we safely assume that Anthony was considered an oddball, misfit, and malcontent in transporting a new story? She was most certainly at the cutting edge of creating a different paradigm than the one into which she'd been born.

What will it take for us to actualize our own full potential while supporting others in doing the same? Are we willing to be seen as oddballs, cranks, cultists, misfits, and malcontents, not unlike Susan B. Anthony, the five women who wrote the Declaration of Sentiments, and Malala Yousafzai? And what about the courage of Meister Eckhart, Rumi, and Hallaj, all of whom were viewed as heretics when they shared publicly their view that each and every one of us carries the seed of God?

The True Spiritual Self

We have witnessed competition and aggression across all countries and cultures. At the same time, many of us are working vigorously to expand and strengthen the possibility of a more compassionate and co-creative culture. How can we support humanity in moving beyond the early stages of survival rooted in fear and insufficiency? Can we take responsibility for how we might be motivated by fear and survival, work to change that way of operating, and support others in doing the same? Can we keep surrendering our fears and anxious imaginations as we focus on becoming our true spiritual selves?

Is what the future holds as fixed and orderly as the mechanistic view of science would have us believe? Or is it actually governed by the universal laws of cause and effect, and therefore influenced and guided by the actions (or non-action) we choose to take now? Isn't much of what happens today a result of past belief systems and behavior? In taking responsibility for our own past history and then letting it all go (finally—once and for all without ruminating and regretting), we will no longer be crippled or compromised by it. Instead, we can use all we've learned from our perceived failures and mistakes as valuable instruction to steer us directly toward the true spiritual self right now, creating and redirecting our way toward a brighter future.

Part of taking responsibility for our individual past and cultivating that brighter future may also involve transcending the patriarchal paradigm by joining with others in taking collective action. This idea has caught fire in some social circuits around the world over the past several years. While patriarchy still largely brands the profiles of governing and corporate interests, movements like #metoo and One Billion Rising—the largest mass action in human history to end violence against women, are shifting the collective mindset-morphic resonance. Somewhere in between traditional role models and emerging variations in self-identity-empowerment/self-belonging, there's a growing desire to move beyond any and all constraints to our own human destiny—whether we are male/female/black/white/orange—or otherwise.

So how do we support each other in creating and becoming the best version of ourselves—both at the micro and macro level? Underneath all of the primal, testosterone-driven, limbic urges for control, competition, aggression, and anger that characterize our patriarchal institutions and incite campaigns for change, there's an archetypal ideal for a Divine Masculine and Divine Feminine. "He" shows up in the form of a conscious, wise intelligence, powerful (as opposed to forceful), authentic, grounded, and content with who he is, having no need to compete, prove his worth, or dictate authority/control over anything or anyone. He already feels worthy and fully self-belonged. He knows how to balance the persuasions of fear-based drives with qualities of the Divine Feminine—unconditional love, compassion, tolerance, patience, wisdom, and gentle strength. When these two forces unite in a global fabric, they have the power to dissolve everything hard, violent, horrific, and obsessed.

I once heard the late David Hawkins, internationally known author and speaker, give a talk on the subject of human consciousness in which he said that we're "primed and ready to expand" into Barbara Marx Hubbard's Universal Human:

> *One connected to the whole of life … awakening from within by a deep heart's desire to express and offer her/his gifts … seeking to join with others to co-create a new and better world…. S/he is a spiritual pioneer who wants to participate in building a more compassionate and co-creative culture … which we do by repeatedly offering love and compassion.*

Groupthink

"Groupthink," a term defined by social psychologist Irving Janis in 1972, is a phenomenon that occurs "when a group makes faulty decisions because of group pressures (usually guided by a charismatic leader) and can result in a deterioration of mental efficiency, reality testing, and moral judgment." Human beings are by nature social animals, shaped by evolution over a four-million-year period to adapt to tribal behavior. This may predispose any of us still operating in survival mode to the influences of groupthink.

In the early development of our civilization, we depended on the tribe to keep us alive. The survival of the individual and her/his immediate family depended on it. Therefore, the drives that cause humans to continue to gather in groups and sub-groups are instinctive, continuing into the 21st century over the course of millions of years.

Sometimes, of course, serious deviations from healthy group dynamics can be devastating. When I entered the psychiatric world in the 1990s, I facilitated various groups in therapy with different demographics. Inevitably, there were challenges, but with good structure and method, most people generally benefited by learning from each other. Nonetheless, when things go awry in a group, whether in the psychiatric world or elsewhere, the groupthink phenomenon can emerge as the primary operative.

The hospital where I was employed admitted patients who had been exposed to everything from satanic ritualistic abuse to drug-related gang violence. It was shocking to learn that such atrocities exist, but even worse to see the unconscionable destruction that groupthink agreements can cause. I witnessed the results of the most deplorable versions of anger, aggression, competition, and violence, and I was repeatedly astounded by how people could be lured and seduced by (or in some cases born into) these tribal horrors.

The groupthink model goes something like this: The guru-gone-south has become a hungry ghost (described in Chapter Seven). This guru thirsts endlessly for power and control, baiting members with false promises of gain, glory, and a sort of twisted salvation once they agree to be involved. These gurus will stop at nothing to promote their radical, dark ideology, often involving the worst kinds of tyranny, anger, and aggression, including rape, murder, or both. Disciples are brain-washed and taught to solicit new candidates by seeking out the vulnerable, naïve, and easily wooed. Naturally, the most susceptible people want to belong to anything that can give them a sense of identity.

While active in my practice, I evaluated a few young men who had been recruited into gangs. I did not see any women or girl gang members, though I know they're out there. These boys all had some basic characteristics in common. They didn't have a sense of belonging to themselves, family, or anything else. They saw themselves as losers and wanted to be a part of something—anything. They were promised lives of meaning and purpose—some by drug lords, who found and solicited them to do their dirty deeds. Rather than discovering any meaning or purpose, they found themselves living nightmares of despair and hopelessness.

There are numerous articles from *The New York Times* citing how Jihadist extremists recruit women to their cause with one consistent pattern: they find the ones who have no sense of belonging to anything—including themselves.

These examples of groupthink represent the darkest side of humanity. Stoking the fire of individual anger can be exponentially strengthened with the momentum of groupthink, unifying forces—however dark and distorted—that create an energy pattern (resonance) with extremely negative consequences.

Taming The Incredible Hulk

When we become angry, we lose our ability to be rational, while taking on a position of righteousness, which is all about forcing our perceptions onto someone else or a group. We can't hear another's position, let alone have tolerance or compassion for them. The more we boil, the more justified we feel in our own position and agenda.

In *How God Changes the Brain*, mentioned earlier, Andrew Newberg discusses the neuroplasticity that occurs through spiritual practices, such as prayer, meditation, and specific relaxation techniques, which can mitigate the sheer force of anger. Some of these practices are believed to bring the practitioner into the presence of God by reducing the obstacles caused by the hyperactivity of the mind. Using these methods can strengthen the anterior cingulate cortex

(ACC), where the qualities of compassion, kindness, love, tolerance, and gratitude are generated. In repeatedly fortifying the ACC with practices that strengthen it, this region of the brain gets the support it needs to balance the effects of the limbic system.

In my defenselessness my safety lies.

—A Course in Miracles

When anger is directed at you, if you can step back rather than react and dissolve into anger yourself, you'll begin to increase your supply of von Economo neurons, which will multiply in the ACC. When you dodge a negative response, you slow down the onslaught of "anger messengers" launched by the amygdala, where the reaction of fight or flight originates. In calming your nervous system by using your breath as a tool, the von Economo neurons develop momentum, eventually providing enough gusto to steady the effect of rowdy neurochemicals cascading from the autonomic nervous system designed to trigger survival mechanisms. When you step away, using your breath to help you unplug from your trigger, you actually create more safety for yourself than you would by defending your position. Defense might only promote a hostile confrontation. The von Economo neurons help you regain your capacity to reason—which is how David was able to win his dual with the giant (Incredible Hulk) Goliath, whose anger caused his own demise.

It takes strength and willpower to step back when your instincts are screaming at you to defend yourself. The spiritual practices that you're cultivating (like in the compassion meditation) will create a new sense of determination. Through Newberg's work, we can see strong evidence to suggest that strengthening the ACC is critical to our expansion into becoming the universal human. By focusing on this region with practices of loving kindness, tolerance, and compassion, we diminish the effects of anger and aggression. When we let go of the Incredible Hulk, we activate the Divine Masculine and Divine Feminine as the primary influences in our lives, while strengthening new paradigms of self-belonging. When we live life as self-belonged beings, we have no need to prove our point or resist someone else's.

Karma — An Explanation for Life Challenges?

I believe the seeming challenge of inequality in people's lives and experiences that I've illuminated in this material begs further explanation, apart from patterns, conditioning, and bloodlines. Buddhists, Hindus, and even some Christian sects (primarily Christian mysticism) explain this inequality as karma, or the law of cause and effect. In the karmic model of life and death, briefly touched on earlier, you can have multiple lifetimes. You choose to return or reincarnate, to work through past actions done to you, by you, or both. If you subscribe to the law of karma, you likely believe that each of us could have lived as men, women, victims, perpetrators, and even as heroes, slaves, or royalty in past lives.

The late Michael Newton had been a practicing psychologist and hypnotherapist for more than forty years when he began to discover an interesting phenomenon while regressing patients in hypnotherapy: some began to report their experiences *between* lives. Since the famed psychiatrist Brian Weiss's discoveries of people going back to *past* lives during hypnosis, regressing people to other lifetimes has become relatively common among practitioners. In some circles, Weiss is considered an expert on the soul's survival after death and one of the first in mainstream medicine to be noted for work in past life regression.

The late Taylor Caldwell, an internationally acclaimed novelist, was a skeptic about re-incarnation, even though the vast and detailed information that came through her certainly convinced others that she had lived before. Eventually, she agreed to undergo a series of hypnotic regressions, where memories of other lives and locales repeatedly emerged. She even spoke in different languages and took on diverse accents under hypnosis. Her experiences set a precedent for Weiss's work.

Newton's work focused on the soul's journey between lives. Following his initial discovery, which happened by accident in a session with a client (similar to Weiss's experience), he regressed hundreds of patients with remarkably similar accounts of what occurs during the "between lives" state. The number of commonalities that his participants shared—including their experience of ten stages during the afterlife, beginning with physical death up to final preparations for reincarnation, is quite profound. According to the accounts of his subjects, which he shared in his book, *Journey of Souls,* we're supported in the afterlife by a wise council and others in the same "soul group," who assist us in deciding how, when, where, and with whom to reincarnate. This decision is based on both our experiences and how we operated in our most recent life, as well as the level of growth we wish to achieve in the next life. Since being trained by Newton in the early 1990s, Linda Backman has conducted her own research with remarkably similar results using independent, professionally obtained data.

If we have all agreed on some level to incarnate on this earth-plane, gathered together in a sort of wisdom school, isn't it possible that we're studying a curriculum co-created by us, our soul team, and God, in order to support our growth, well-being, and ultimate freedom? In terms of my own curriculum, couldn't it have been designed to help me eliminate my maladaptive patterns with men? If so, my relationship with Richard, as well as the relationships that came before, provided a valuable template for my learning.

151

When Richard didn't show up at the hospital while I was stretched out on that gurney, I felt betrayed by his actions because I was looking at the situation through the lens of projection, blame, and victimhood. If, during those moments when I was most triggered, I could have stepped back and witnessed my part in casting the episode, I might have moved beyond the pattern. I might have considered the possibility of a karmic knot that I could unravel with him (and others) by turning the focus on myself and changing my own behavior, rather than trying to change anyone else.

In the section to follow, I'll share a powerful practice, which has had proven results in supporting such a shift, and certainly has helped me to shift mine.

Ho'oponopono

Forgiveness is not an act of altruism. It is an act of getting your soul back.

—Matthew Fox

In 1975, a Hawaiian sage known as Morrnah Nalamaku Simeona began to modify the traditional Kahana practice of Ho'oponopono, which is believed to resolve subconscious beliefs caused by painful memories. In her own words: "Ho'oponopono is a profound gift that allows one to develop a working relationship with the inner Divine and to learn to ask that in each moment, our errors in thought, word, deed, or action be cleansed. The process is essentially about complete freedom from the past."

Simeona's version of the ancient ritual was influenced by a combination of Eastern, Christian, and Hawaiian traditions, offering that you must have a "working partnership with the subconscious,

conscious, and super-conscious minds, together with inner Divinity, in order to recognize your true identity" or the true spiritual self. Eventually, prior to her death in 1992, Simeona was invited to perform trainings of her Ho'oponopono practice for the United Nations, Johns Hopkins Medical School, and the University of Hawaii, as well as various business and religious organizations in fourteen countries.

How does this process work, and what does it mean to recognize your true identity? Simeona explained: "We are the sum total of our experiences. It is the emotions, tied to our memories of events, which affect us now." This brings to mind our discussions about the amygdala's influence on our emotions, which can diminish reasoning in the prefrontal cortex. Consistent with Bruce Lipton's findings, Simeona taught that every memory and experience is recorded in our subconscious data bank. She believed that the process of Ho'oponopono could help to neutralize triggers, purifying one's inner self.

Ihaleakala Hew Len, who was mentored by Simeona, is a former chief psychologist at Hawaii State Hospital's ward for the criminally insane. His work on the ward provides a potent example of the positive effects of Ho'oponopono. Thirty years ago, when Hew Len came on board, the unit's patients were in lockdown and diagnosed with extreme mental conditions, including severe cases of sociopathic and antisocial behavior. Because of the dire situation on the ward, the hospital gave Hew Len wide berth to alter traditional therapy.

He canceled all clinical sessions, never attended rounds or staff meetings, and didn't speak to patients other than to greet them in the hall. Instead, he worked quietly in his office, writing down the name of each patient or holding their medical record in his hands. He then proceeded to take on their pains and problems as if they were his own (noticing if he was upset by their behavior or the conditions, which resulted in their diagnosis of criminal insanity), and worked on healing those issues within himself. The following is the practice he used:

> *Dear Divine, I love you. (This statement sets the tone for the exchange.) Please correct in me any aberrations of behavior that I witness in this other. I too have the potential to act on subconscious memories that trigger my reactions, and perhaps have done so many times in this lifetime or in previous lives. Please forgive me. I am sorry. Thank you for clearing me of judgment while helping me to see this person in her/his original state of Divine perfection. Thank you for removing all of my own thoughts and memories that could manifest in anything harmful to me or another.*

Over the course of his four-year tenure on the ward, Hew Len systematically helped to heal the entire unit and everything else along with it—even down to the paint on the wall, which apparently wouldn't stick prior to his arrival. At the end of his time there, the mood and atmosphere on the ward had changed so dramatically that all but two of the patients were released. When the two remaining were relocated, the entire unit was eliminated. In taking radical responsibility for himself, focusing only on clearing negativity in his own thoughts and memories, he influenced healing for a population that was seen as hopeless.

The underlying operative in Ho'oponopono is that we're all connected in the human family, and each of us has the potential for the most altruistic, benevolent behavior, as well as the worst and most malevolent—and everything in between. Furthermore, because we're all linked in one way or another (through the morphogenetic field), when I lovingly invoke the Divine's participation in helping me clear my own errors, including what triggers me and my judgments of others as wrong, the positive effects of my intention reverberate to others.

In *The Synchronicity Key*, David Wilcock says our thoughts about others actually create "tunnels" connecting us to them. "Anytime you have a thought about someone, this tunnel is automatically created in the Source Field (hidden intelligence) between us and that person, and photons (particles representing electromagnetic energy) begin passing through it." If this is so, then is it possible that during the practice of Ho'oponopono, your intent to clear any harmful thoughts and memories caused by another supports both of you in the healing process? It would appear that the work of Hew Len offers living proof.

How will you know if your practice or version of Ho'oponopono is working? When you are less and less bothered by the person or event that notified you of your need for clearing in the first place. Eventually, you'll completely unplug from the charge, reestablishing your connection to the Divine. As you collaborate with the Source Field to polish up your foggy lens, you'll see through the eyes of the Beloved, who takes a radically compassionate view. The happy side-effect of this process is that everything and everyone else associated with the issue will benefit. Of course, your main concern will be to concentrate on whatever is haywire in *you*. When you fully operate from your foundation of pure potential, you recognize that you aren't here to save anyone, but just to release your own soul from memories and behaviors that don't support your growth and expansion.

Having used the practice of Ho'oponopono for more than a decade now, I can bear witness to its powerful effects. If I can remember to use it when I feel upset by another, I can take responsibility for my own propensity to act as an offender and unravel the karmic residue between us. Inevitably, any hesitation in my willingness to take full responsibility for my own deeds and thoughts will result in a delay of healing, which is evidenced by my prolonged recovery from my failed relationship with Richard.

Also, the more feeling and authenticity we put into the practice, the better the result. At times, when I'm thrown off balance by someone, I actually get excited about the opportunity to clear a pattern or untie a karmic knot that I may have perpetuated for lifetimes. As a human still living in a physical body, I'm not always inclined to look at myself when I let those anger messengers take hold—sometimes perpetuating my own misery.

Since learning about the technique of Ho'oponopono and Hew Len's work, I have given some workshops on the practice. In one of these, I was unaware that a participant had actually been employed at the State Hospital of Hawaii at the time of Len's tenure. The man maintained anonymity during the day and surprised me after my presentation with the gift of confirming my findings. Was his participation that day a coincidence or an act of Divine synchronicity?

Reflections from the Road

Only those who dare drive the world forward.

—Anonymous

Even though on many levels, we are an adaptive species, once we've agreed on a certain way of being as a collective, it's hard for us to change. Yet, we can see the huge difference some have made by daring to drive the world forward—Sufi and Christian mystics alike; statesmen such as Washington, Jefferson, and Lincoln; healers like Morrnah Simeona and Hew Len; and women, like Susan B. Anthony and Malala Yousafzai.

It takes courage and resilience to recognize the need to clean up our lives—and then to go on about the business of doing it—one self-belonged moment at a time.

That you're attracted to this material makes you a torchbearer, too. It doesn't matter what flavor of hero you decide to become, only that you start by a devotion to yourself and the path for expanding your own potential. You have patiently listened as I've continued to share parts of my journey—perhaps sometimes pausing to interject your own thoughts in this intimate conversation we've been having. Believe me, I can hear you—shouting out your victories, as well as your frustrations and agonies. And because of these triumphs, frustrations, and agonies of yours, I'm able to stay true to my own path. Knowing you're out there fortifies my stamina and strength as I go forward in my attempts to make a difference for myself, while hoping to help others along the way.

I fully believe that we can transcend our cravings for the next dopamine hit in whatever form those cravings may show up. When we're brave enough to stare down any maladaptive behavior that drives us, we can be assured that we've got what it takes to stop satisfying our deepest longings with anything other than digging in that narrow place. Eventually, we'll realize that our inner yearnings will only yield to our practice of self-belonging.

It takes courage and resilience to recognize the need to clean up our lives—and then to go on about the business of doing it—one self-belonged moment at a time. Once you're willing to hold your feet to the fire, something very interesting begins to happen. It doesn't appear in one news-breaking moment or with a flash of instant gratification. Instead, it's a very different kind of experience—new and altogether unfamiliar to us as a gang of former pleasure-seekers.

One fine day, you'll wake up and realize how dearly you enjoy the colors of the flowers that decorate the sidewalk as you walk to work. Feelings of deep gratitude will wash over you as you stand in your local yoga studio, appreciating the space, the teacher, and the firm feeling of your feet on the ground. You'll take more delight in greeting the barista at your favorite café—even more than the coffee she prepares for you. You'll recognize a particularly vivid sunrise, when the sky is awash with magical hues that you've never noticed before in quite the same way.

On this fine day, you'll realize that for some time now, you've been utterly enchanted with the little things in your life—none of which has anything to do with pleasure and everything to do with happiness. What's the difference? The former is about getting high. The latter is a stable, constant wave that runs in the river of your being. And all you have to do to experience it is to be grateful for each moment of now—regardless of what it may seem to be delivering.

Happiness isn't something you get; it's something you have. How would I know? Remember: I'm your personal research project.

Practice: Ho'oponopono:

Make miracles out of grievances.

—A Course in Miracles

In addition to the personal Ho'oponopono invocation above, Morrnah Nalamaku Simeona offered this more general prayer:

Divine Creator, father, mother, son, daughter, as one....
If I, my family, relatives and ancestors have offended
you, your family, relatives and ancestors by thoughts,
words, deeds and actions from the beginning of our
creation to the present, we ask your forgiveness....
Let this cleanse, purify, release, cut all the negative
memories, blocks, energies, and vibrations and
transmute these unwanted energies to pure light....
And it is done.

As we continue our journey into self-belonging, the practice of Ho'oponopono offers one more vehicle for surveying the inner land-scape—a tangible tool to release your triggers, embrace forgiveness, and retrieve your soul.

* Practice *

Please create your own version of Ho'oponopono,
practice it as often as you're upset by another, and
watch as grievances turn to miracles—repeatedly.

In Chapter Nine, I'll show how resolving some of my own grievances has generated miraculous results.

NINE

Black Widow and Captain America Share the Airspace

*

I want to know if you know how to melt into that fierce heat of living—falling toward the center of your longing.

—David Whyte

After an encounter in the Denver International Airport, I had an entertaining dream that I was accomplishing superhero tasks like an Avenger in the Marvel comic series—sort of a Black Widow/Captain America combo. Maybe the incident that preceded it could explain what kicked my subconscious into superhuman mode.

While waiting to board my flight and in blissful anticipation of returning to my little nest after a long journey, I glanced at the monitor and was jolted momentarily breathless by a glaring abbreviation. It appeared to be a representation of Richard's name waitlisted for an upgrade. I immediately rationalized why it couldn't possibly refer to the one human on the entire planet I didn't want to see. *Even if he did travel, he wouldn't be eligible for an upgrade*, I judged.

Nevertheless, I felt myself go from mild anxiety to full-blown panic in less than a nanosecond. How was I going to escape this potentially calamitous development? A stream of options raced through my head like a runaway rollercoaster.

In full-on fight or flight mode, I went with the latter option: *flee*. I immediately escaped to the only off-limits-to-Richard location that came to mind—the ladies' room. Settling into my temporary safety zone and protected from the potential ground zero situation, I made weak attempts to persuade myself that the abbreviated name couldn't belong to *him*. I wasn't convinced.

The clock rolled on. While glaring at my glassy-eyed reflection in the mirror, I realized I was down to two choices. Either I would spend the night on the floor of the loo or head for home. I recruited my strength and strode out of the bathroom with Black Widow/Captain America resolve, fortified with Gustave Thibon's insights shared earlier: "Beware of mirages. Do not run or fly away in order to get free: rather dig in the narrow place which has been given you; you will find God there and everything.... Vanity runs, love digs."

Time to dig. Upon approaching gate 83, Richard's unmistakable head of hair glared at me like a neon light. There he was, decked out in swank linen pants and complementary suede jacket. This stylish attire had replaced the familiar weathered, worn-out jeans and Izod shirt, layered on top of the signature-Richard-colored tee. His classy new travel-look clearly promoted him into the upgrade category. Damn it. He was dashing.

Without hesitation, I walked over and stood beside him. When he looked up, his crimson-rust tan instantly washed out into a sort of ashen-clay gray. I had my first flash of compassion in that moment. (The poor bastard hadn't had my advantage of preparation.) I was quick to come up with a strategy to lighten up the scene, removing my Avenger mask while doing a serious love dig per Thibon.

My granddaughter immediately came to mind. "There's someone I'd like you to meet," I said confidently (attempting to disguise my

161

vulnerability). I handed him my phone so he could scroll through my endless photo stream of this precious treasure in my life. It was a good strategy: I was strengthened by her sweet, sparkly smile.

After that, I treated him like an old friend and kept the conversation light. We avoided any topic related to our history together, with a couple of exceptions. I told Richard that he had been my greatest teacher. He was quick to receive the revelation as a compliment. Perhaps in so doing he hadn't considered the lessons I'd counted as particularly instructive. It didn't matter. He went on to say that I had taught him how to love. However poetic that remark seemed to be in the moment, I didn't acknowledge it. What the hell was that supposed to mean, anyway? Was he now loving someone else, who was benefiting from *my* instruction? I wasn't going to bite on that familiar bait. Instead, I just let my upset diffuse, while redirecting the conversation elsewhere. (Well done, if I do say so myself.)

The plane continued to be delayed. How was I going to extricate myself from this situation in a gate area the size of a postage stamp? *Let it go*, I inwardly demanded. Mercifully, just as we were called to board, someone we both knew struck up a conversation, gushing about how great it was to see us together—blah blah blah.

When we finally boarded and were seated separately, my heart rate returned to normal. As we climbed into the clouds, I marveled at the beauty of the setting sun, painting the sky a brilliant heart-pink as the little jet skimmed over the mountaintops and soared into a heaven of my own making. It was real and palpable. I was belonging to myself. I was loving my life. I was thriving—*alone*. I would soon descend into the sacred village that I dearly loved, where I live in solitude. My heart burst with an indescribable sense of appreciation, wonder, and awe.

Upon landing, I accepted Richard's offer to drive me home rather than take a cab. I had nestled nicely into my self-belonging skin, while quietly reflecting on all the milestones, however subtle, that had led me to that ground. Upon arriving, I declined his offer to carry my forty-nine-pound bag up the stairs and over my threshold. To me, my refusal represented two significant breakthroughs: the first, that I was more than willing to do the heavy lifting for my own life, and the second, I was successfully maintaining boundaries with this man, who I'd previously been unable to refuse. No matter how dashing Richard looked or what he said, he wouldn't be permitted to cross into the sacred space I call home. Did he get the unspoken message? I don't know. What's important is that I did—yet one more time.

I later thought about all the occasions when he had walked away from me, aloof, non-committal, and painfully distant—in the absence of any discussion about when we would see each other again. I let his passivity cause me near intolerable anguish and despair. He vigorously resisted making any plans, and I vigorously resisted not having any. Here's the irony: I have now come to a place in my life when I don't like making plans either—and my open-ended farewell was an obvious indicator. Would we ever see each other again? I didn't care in the least—not in a snippety sort of way—just simple apathy.

When I ascended the staircase to my little tree-house sanctuary, I felt an overwhelming sense of relief and gratitude. I had walked away from Richard—again. Only on this occasion, there was no fire, no charge, no regret, no anger, and no longing. Perhaps most significant of all, after everything I had been through with this person, *I had dropped my resistance to him*. My insoluble problem of being in an impossible relationship with someone I didn't think I could leave had lost its urgency. I *had* left; I *had* survived. The life urge has taken precedence over any lingering temptation to be seduced back into a circular treadmill of repeated pain dotted with intermittent pleasure with this man.

Pretzels

As you know, I describe my former self as someone fully afflicted with the *Cinderella Complex*, per Colette Dowling—or the good woman syndrome. I believe Jane Fonda, actress and activist, captured the essence of that syndrome perfectly during her 2003 speech at the National Women's Leadership Summit in Washington D.C.:

> *See, although I've always been financially independent, and professionally and socially successful, behind the closed doors of my personal life I was still turning myself into a pretzel so I'd be loved by an alpha male. I thought if I didn't become whatever he wanted me to be, I'd be alone, and then, I wouldn't exist.... Early on in my third act I found my voice and, in the process, I have ended up alone ... but not really. You see, I'm with myself.*

Here is a woman who has been perceived by many as wildly successful—looks, fame, wit, wisdom, money, the list is endless. Doesn't Jane Fonda have it all? Yet, she admits to having had this pretzel problem, which I have spent the majority of my adult life and several thousand words trying to unravel, both in this book and the last one. Now, you'd think that those of us who might funnel ourselves into the pretzel category would be limited to financially dependent women with no identity at all aside from their man. Fonda certainly disproves that theory, as does my own story.

Women have made some strides since the days of Susan B. Anthony and the launching of the Women's Liberation Movement by Gloria Steinem in the 1970s. As mentioned in Chapter Seven, more women than men are graduating from some of the most prestigious

American law schools, and there are now more women physicians than men in the US.

Even so, despite all of our developing brilliance on how to become professionals and tackle the work world, while dressed to the nines in our high-heeled shoes and crisp white collars, many of us are still perplexed by the insoluble problem of how to snag and keep that alpha male (one possible explanation for wearing that remarkably uncomfortable footwear).

Didn't Fonda hit the true crux of the issue plaguing so many women with her honest, vulnerable, and bold revelation about fearing that she wouldn't exist in the absence of being loved by an alpha male? I believe this mindset involves deep-seated stuff rooted in the old part of the female psyche—intricately entwined with a multitude of other conditions and complications.

Isn't it our moral imperative, both for ourselves and for each other, to challenge and transcend an outdated operating system that no longer serves us? How can I alchemize my ironclad past, burdened with subconscious, habituated patterns, into a future of golden possibilities? As discussed in *Happily Ever After … Right Now*, we don't need the brute to save us from the threats of the world anymore. We have the tools and the wherewithal to save ourselves. We've proven that not only can we exist without an alpha male, we can thrive. And aren't we more positioned to join with others who are also thriving—including the glorious men who are themselves coming into wholeness—when we're operating at optimal levels? What would we look like if we were to greet the world with our hearts opened and arms outstretched, rather than twisting ourselves into whatever we think we ought to be in order to be okay for him (or for our prospects)? Furthermore, is it his fault that we do this? Is it the fault of the patriarchal culture into which we were born?

If you do have a partner, or you plan to have one in the future, wouldn't he be grateful to not have to be the central focus of your universe or live up to your standards of Prince Charming? When you quit focusing on him as the answer, don't you free up incredible amounts of energy to live the life of your dreams—with or without him?

Secrets and Lies Revisited

My own twists and turns are now fading memories, but still emerge once in a while, prompted by ordinary life. While recently putting together a dinner party for some friends, I flashed back to a few summers ago when I volunteered to entertain several of Richard's colleagues. (By now, you may have figured out that Richard and I never lived together.) The event took place at his house. My home is in the high alpine country, and his is down the valley about a thirty-minute drive through a windy canyon. I purchased all the groceries, prepared the food, and made two trips to cater the meal in full-blown-over-functioning-good-girl-mode. On my second trip down, I had taken a change of clothes, planning to shower there and spend the night.

Richard waltzed in minutes before the guests arrived. Greeted by an adoring partner, who'd prepared a sparkling clean house decorated with flowers, candles, and a plethora of goodies, he uttered a single comment. I'd just spritzed myself with his favorite scent.

"Your perfume is too strong," he barked, with a look of irritation nearing disgust. That's it. That's all he said. Not "Thank you for all you have done." Not "Wow! Everything looks terrific." Not "This must have been a lot of work." Not "Do I owe you anything for the groceries?" Nope. None of that.

Slack-jaw stunned, I stood in a state of paralysis. Before I could catch my breath, the doorbell's alarm sounded a shrill warning that the guests were arriving. A clean getaway would now be impossible.

166

Richard's searing words evoked flashbacks of my father's frequent disrespect and similar dismissal of my mother, who'd prepared countless meals for his business associates, entertaining tirelessly on his behalf. How had I let history repeat itself here? I stuffed that thought, together with my horror and hurt, smeared on my good woman happy face, and stood by my man for the duration of the evening.

Halfway into the night as I worked my ass off while Richard sat on his, I had another bombshell blast. Joann, the wife of Richard's colleague, Christian, privately shared the second shocker of the evening—something that had occurred a few months prior. By her report, Richard had premeditated a plan to stop off at Betty's home in Denver (his former fiancé mentioned in the prologue) on the way back from a business trip that he and Christian had taken together. Therefore, Christian wouldn't be able to ride with Richard as previously planned.

This carefully disguised meeting with Betty explained Richard's six-hour delay to *my* house that night, which he had passed off with a lame excuse. When he did appear at close to 2:00 a.m., he was unusually exuberant and loving—bearing gifts accompanied by plenty of endearments—all part of a scheme orchestrated to eclipse the inconvenience I'd allowed him to cause by his unacceptable tardiness. As clever Richard knew quite well, all the nail-biting moments that I'd spent thinking he was in a ditch somewhere that night were quickly forgotten, obscured by his sappy sweet talk.

After the guests finally left, I confronted him with the information Joann had shared. He sheepishly admitted having gone by to see how Betty was doing and turned purple while claiming he'd made a bad call. That was his only comment. Instead of finally seizing the opportunity to take my leave (long overdue following the perfume incident), I headed to the kitchen like a good wife (only I wasn't a wife). Aside from banging around a few dishes here and there, I was silent and passive—never mind what was cooking in my internal boiler room. Artfully, Richard manipulated his way back into my good graces with loving gestures and endearments. It was these tender times with him that I came to crave and cherish—the ones after he'd been the "bad boy" and wanted to make up. I clung to that sweet-talking gentle version of Richard, believing every time he morphed into that persona—one among his multiple others, that it would stick. Of course, it never did.

Thriving

Was my involvement with Richard a symptom of a behavioral addiction? I believe that it undoubtedly was. Have I recovered? I believe I have, which I say with caution and humility. Here is what I can observe about my progress: Not only am I no longer powerless over my craving, but I no longer *experience* any noticeable craving or longing for another to make me feel whole and complete. I'm learning more and more how to regulate my emotional highs and lows, a process that I expect to refine as long as I'm vertical.

In fact, I'll let you in on a little secret: just after I started writing this chapter several months ago, I was repeatedly tested, not only with Richard, but in other arenas of my world on this thriving business. As you may have noticed occasionally in your own life, when you declare and announce that you're finally ready to receive all the glory that life has to offer, the Universe will inevitably send along multiple tests just to make sure you mean it.

As I've mentioned, Richard and I both live in a small mountain community, driving the same narrow corridor that connects one side of the valley to the other. We hike the same trails, shop at the same markets, and based on our mutual interests, often attend many of the same events. So, in addition to the Black Widow/Captain America adventure at the Denver airport, Richard has continued to surface and resurface in my world like the bear I encountered in the woods. Even though my mind knew they were both around, my heart and my body were still wired to react each time they reappeared—despite all of my bold proclamations about not caring when or if that happened.

Therefore, in the midst of my healing, during the days, nights, months, and years that I've spent letting go of my attachment to the pain/pleasure cycle and the relationships that represented that dance, I've suffered setbacks and surprises. Just as alcoholics sometimes do. Just as overeaters sometimes do. We are only human after all. In my case, I couldn't always create physical space between me and my nemesis. It wasn't a matter of clearing all the wine, pills, or ice cream from the premises, but rather navigating the same narrow territory as the walking, talking, roaming Richard.

I absolutely did start by going from one nanosecond to the next in creating those new circuits underneath the skull of my resistance. My pattern had been to keep repeating the familiar cycle of pain and pleasure—the latest example being my part in how Richard and I behaved together. Suddenly, in one very significant, flashing moment (prompted by a dog, Betty, and the police), I decided to quit participating in that cycle. Fortunately, that final jolt was permanently branded in my brain. That awareness stayed with me for hours. The hours turned into days, the days morphed into months, and the months into years. Did I almost give in? Yes—on a few occasions. Only something was there to advise me not to—the subtle, profound stirring that's utterly intangible and completely the most real of all things. It sustained and supported me in strengthening the indomitable will, which kept me from caving. It was, of course, the silent voice of self-belonging—the Indwelling God.

What I've learned is that *awareness* is the ticket to thriving. When you have the courage to become aware of whatever has kept you from actualizing your full potential, there's an underlying support system that wakes up from dormancy and informs your self-regulation system to kick in, while systematically showing you how to pay attention to the life urge. It supports you in merging your conscious mind with your subconscious databank—every waking moment. It will do this in a variety of ways—through your bodily aches and pains, through even the slightest twinge of stress and strain, and quite often through what shows up in your dream state, providing messages about what's going on down under. I have found that keeping a journal to record my dreams has been helpful in unraveling clues and memos delivered from my subconscious. In writing things out, I've often been able to identify themes.

For example, my Avenger dream might have been affirming to me that I've adopted a more courageous way of operating in the past few years.

Over time, the earth under my feet seems more unwavering, whether about Richard, health, finances, or any of the other endless uncertainties that can stalk me in my weaker moments. The unsteady turf has gradually begun to yield to my awareness and to the discipline that rises out of devotion—not only to the Indwelling God, but to my rigorous schedule of yoga, hiking, meditation, prayer, contemplation, inspirational reading, spiritual direction, and a tenacious attitude of "everything is always working out for me, no matter how it looks." To the best of my ability, I've remained disciplined, detached, and obedient to my process, while letting go of what the outcome might be. I've continued to focus on what I want and surrender the result, while feeling gratitude and appreciation for my many blessings. Am I always able to stay on the self-belonging path? No. Of course not; I'm human. But with awareness, I can jump back on, pick up where I left off, and remember that my commitment to growing my soul has a cumulative effect.

My practices have fortified me through all the inevitable stages of grief (anger, denial, depression, bargaining, and acceptance), continually strengthening my self-regulation circuits. I have not only survived, but transcended some unhealthy patterns. I've come to belong to myself to such a degree that I could never again allow someone to crush all manner of logic in me. And while in the process of strengthening my commitment to self-belong, I've been constantly nurtured by the Indwelling God, exponentially broadening my outlook and propelling me into a whole new stratosphere of unlimited possibilities.

Reflections on *Cinderella*

As I move into Act III of my own life, here's what I can share in reflecting on a *Cinderella*-influenced past, while repeatedly examining ways to reimagine my future: first off, I owe any victory or success fully and completely to the Indwelling God, who has always been available to harmonize with my creative genius—a genius we all possess. I just had to finally allow that harmony to reverberate through my blood, bones, heart, and soul. It has been a process—one that I don't believe is ever finished, nor neat and tidy. I see this call to Grace as a sort of promotion from spiritual childhood into adulthood—wisely described by Scott Peck in *The Road Less Traveled*. Of course, as we grow into adulthood, we know if we keep eating ice cream for breakfast, lunch, and dinner, there will be consequences (bummer).

From time to time, while pondering my own hero's journey and some of the fears I've been able to overcome along the way, I have tremendous compassion for myself for having endured the consequences of buying into a belief system of dependency. Being alone or abandoned used to mean death to women—and in some instances, it still does.

If things are going to come into balance, don't we women have to do our part—not by trying to control anything, but by bringing forth the best version of ourselves? In order to do this, don't we have to love ourselves to the degree that we actually believe we *deserve* to be in reciprocal relationships? We can start (or continue) cultivating self-love by diving down into that narrow place within where we will find God and everything. When immersed in that love, there's no need to go looking for it in other places. And the irony is that when focusing on our relationship with the Divine, love *will* show up—*everywhere*.

Detachment and Surrender

The future holds limitless possibilities as you step into the field of your own belonging. In so doing, you will continue to broaden your outlook, where you will be guided into much more expansive worlds than you've previously known. All the while, you'll cultivate and refine a different emotional standard by strengthening your self-regulation circuits. Together with your faith, these circuits will support you in moving into greater states of surrender and detachment. You'll be less likely to see the external conditions of your life as a barometer for how you feel. Instead, you'll be more inclined to rely on the Indwelling God. Sometimes, this faith of yours will take you right to the very edge of your tolerance. Even so, if you can hang onto that faith, mustard seed by mustard seed, mingled with some genuine gratitude, you will invariably marvel at who and what keeps showing up to join and assist you.

Your soul has agreed to come here to overcome limitation—to transcend things that have hurt you or kept you stuck.

Of course, all of this faith you've cultivated, accompanied by a willingness to become better acquainted with the Indweller, is cumulative and will continue to serve you even in moments when you worry that all of your hard-earned coping strategies have evaporated. *They haven't.* So, you can tell David Whyte, who wrote the line at the beginning of this chapter, that you most definitely *do* know how to "melt into that fierce heat of living," for you have met your longing head on. And what you've come to understand is that you won't be able to dislodge your craving if you continue to perceive it as a problem. Because then, it's an insoluble dilemma.

Instead, if you let the longing simply *notify* you with awareness to switch your focus to the life urge, it will lose its urgency, and a higher or wider interest will take its place.

Rod Stryker, mentioned in Chapter Two, offers that we're all part of a Divine Intelligence (the Source Field or God), which supports and holds us together. He says there's an order underneath the chaotic surface of things, both for us individually, as well as collectively. He suggests that when you are in alignment with that order, you'll be happy. If you aren't in alignment, you won't be happy. When your deepest driving desire is in harmony with your dharma code—that unique expression you and only you can offer to the world—you will thrive. You have something that no one else on earth can deliver. Therefore, what you're willing to do in order to uncover that dharma code and then take action upon will ultimately shape your destiny— and the planet's—right along with you.

Your soul has agreed to come here to overcome limitation—to transcend things that have hurt you or have kept you stuck. As I've said, one sure method for doing so is to continue examining your attachments or what you might be resisting. When you're willing to do whatever it takes to pry yourself loose from what binds you and let go of your resistance to whatever or whomever you're holding hostage as a villain—metaphorically or otherwise, you'll start to experience boundless freedom. I know because I have tasted that freedom by examining my own resistance and attachments.

Agendas, Faith, and Letting Go of the Cinderella Complex

I believe the relationship conundrum and the problems we have as a civilization related to that conundrum are caused by a variety of factors: karma, conditioning, patterns, bloodlines/ancestry, and archetypes—all of which have contributed to our status as a species. This is good news because all you have to do to upgrade your own status is to stare down what isn't working in your life, be willing to take responsibility for your part, and let go of whatever or whoever no longer serves you.

If you're a relationship addict who finds herself repeatedly attracted to the wrong guy, as was the case for me, you'll only be able to find your dharma—your life path—when you stop doing whatever has kept you distracted from your self-belonging soul. If you're willing to put up and shut up to keep him happy, you've locked yourself into your own cage.

Susan B. Anthony, Jane Fonda, and Malala Yousafzai have something in common. They *have* been willing to stare down what wasn't working in their lives and do whatever it took to free themselves from the noose of fear, while helping others to do the same. I suspect some measure of discipline, self-regulation, detachment, obedience, and surrender were all part of the process.

As for me, I am fiercely committed to my self-belonging, as I support you, dear reader, in doing the same.

Recap of Tools for Self Belonging

*

What I've learned so far on programming for Self-Actualization/Realization

Take responsibility for your life, your issues, your challenges, and your victories, while avoiding the trap of shame and blame.

Examine the lessons behind your errors so that you don't have to repeat them.

Recognize when you have an agenda, and let it go. Focus on what you can offer rather than what you can get.

Make a daily appointment with God. Show up and *listen* to what S/He's got for you to ponder. Then it's your turn to talk. Morph your appointment into a disciplined practice of meditation, contemplation, and inspirational reading.

If you aren't exercising, eating consciously, or avoiding weird chemicals and substances that don't belong in your body, it's time to turn that around.

Dig in the "narrow place within." Don't try to satisfy conditions in your life in order to be free and happy. Rather, focus on the positive aspects of any situation, avoiding negativity — it really isn't that hard, and then watch in wonder as things continue to shift in an upward direction.

Notice when you're swimming upstream, metaphorically or otherwise. Change direction to downstream.

Be committed to self-regulation — discipline, detachment, obedience, and surrender. Catch your emotional highs and lows, and learn to balance them.

God has your back, so face your fears. Keeping those daily, hourly, minute-by-minute appointments helps.

Open the back door of your heart to yourself. Then, open the front door of your heart to the world. Have gratitude for everything. *Everything*. When you feel yourself slipping into the below-neutral zone of your emotional scale—the bottom being downright depressed and the top being exhilarating joy, see what you can do to inch your way up by reaching for better feeling thoughts. Again, gratitude is your key here.

If you have more pain than gain in any relationship, and you have done your best to negotiate reasonable changes, you know what to do: either accept the situation and person as is or walk— *maybe run*. Before you run, however, check in with yourself to see if there are any traces of dependency that have caused you to believe it's the other's job to make you happy. Remember: accessing happiness is an internal job—the whole identifying your dharma code thing and all.

Be aware of your growth-inhibiting patterns. Abstain from behaviors that have the potential to lock you into the pain/ pleasure syndrome, including thoughts and substances.

If you mess up, have compassion for yourself, and begin again. Let the past go. You have zero power there. You can have all the do-overs you want, however exhausting, but avoid the mess up in the first place by amping up your awareness and those self-regulation circuits.

See if you can accept your flaws, and then be sure to identify and celebrate your strengths. The downer days give you something to reach for, keeping life interesting. The sun consistently shines in south Maui—with only occasional afternoon showers. People who live there often go to the other side of the island just to experience changes in the weather. We are curious beings, who actually seek out contrast. It helps us recognize what we *don't* want, so we can identify what we *do* want.

And ... *lighten up*.

176

RECAP OF TOOLS FOR SELF BELONGING

Epilogue
The Inner Place of Grace
*

Go to the Limits of Your Longing

God speaks to each of us as he makes us,
then walks with us silently out of the night.

These are the words we dimly hear:

You, sent out beyond your recall,
go to the limits of your longing.
Embody me.

Flare up like a flame
and make big shadows I can move in.

Let everything happen to you: beauty and terror.
Just keep going. No feeling is final.
Don't let yourself lose me.

Nearby is the country they call life.
You will know it by its seriousness.

Give me your hand.

— Rainer Maria Rilke

Outgrowing Insoluble Problems—Reflections on Your Personal Research Project

Jung's quote (shared in chapter one):

> *All the greatest and most important problems of life are fundamentally insoluble.... They can never be solved, but only outgrown. This "outgrowing" proved on further investigation to require a new level of consciousness. Some higher or wider interest appeared on the patient's horizon, and through this broadening of his or her outlook the insoluble problem lost its urgency. It was not solved logically in its own terms but faded when confronted with a new and stronger life urge.*

While writing this manuscript, I have used my relationship with Richard to illustrate a variety of what I thought were insoluble problems—and not one of them lost its urgency until I gave up trying to fix what was unfixable. A significant part of the process was taking one hundred percent responsibility for my part in what went down between us. In doing so, I expanded my study and research into ancient human wiring in an effort to discover why we humans still keep reverting to our outdated programming. I wanted to know more about how to strengthen the neural platforms that fortify God/consciousness/awareness that will turn us in the right direction into more expansive ways of operating. I continue to learn that implementing the practices that will support us in taking that turn requires determination, faith, will, and above all—*love*. You have to believe more in God and yourself than you do in the thing you thought was going to save you (in my case, Richard—and some others who preceded him), from your fears, longing, and anxious imagination.

And as you do, one fine day you will wake up and realize that your insoluble problems have lost their urgency—as I am discovering.

Recall Andrew Newberg's findings in *How God Changes the Brain* with spiritual practices. For me, engaging in those spiritual practices doesn't produce the kind of reward I've gotten out of the pain/pleasure cycle. Instead, in my own healing process, there has been an entirely different kind of gratification. It has come along slowly, gradually, and incrementally, which I presume is how we build and stabilize the neurotransmitter networks that will steadily override the limbic system—replete with its fight or flight responses and dopamine-driven desire. And I suspect that those updated grid-systems in our brains will sustain the new level of consciousness that Jung talked about, merging the subconscious and the conscious mind. As that happens, a sort of quiet, gentle knowing emerges, repeatedly assuaging your unnecessary fears, as that knowing quietly and consistently reminds you that *love* is an ever-present constant in your life that you can't separate yourself from.

Therefore, no matter what's going on in your external world (he isn't calling, doesn't show up, or whatever else might have the potential to freak you out), you aren't only okay, *but profoundly so*. Remarkably, as mentioned in Chapter One, it was such an awareness that strengthened Naj so many years ago even in the stark, institutional environment where he lived for two full years entirely deprived of any human love.

As for what happened between Richard and me, my unresolved fears—for which I repeatedly attempted to find an external solution rather than turning to God—triggered all of *his* unresolved fears (or vice-versa). So instead of camouflaging them, as we'd hoped to do in the relationship, we exposed them, like raw, gaping wounds. Our patterns repeatedly collided, and in the midst of the ongoing turmoil, we forgot that God could walk us silently out of the night.

Our challenges were insoluble because we kept trying to resolve them with impossible solutions, wanting the other to change. Whether or not the relationship would have been sustainable if we'd used it as a spiritual practice, which would have fit in quite nicely with our mutual goals for spiritual development, we could have chosen to grow in the presence of the relationship without the need to alter the other. Unfortunately, it wasn't like that, so no amount of therapy, of which we had plenty, was going to help. Of course, as I've said before and can't emphasize enough, I didn't really start to heal until I was willing to look at how I was participating in the unconscious setup that Richard and I played out together—ping-ponging back and forth in a classic pain/pleasure paradigm.

Once I pried myself loose from him, I needed resources to support my commitment to change. Over the years, I'd collected and cultivated many tools and was motivated to research more methods for personal and collective transformation as I put the words to paper on these pages. In my recovery, I had to learn to self-regulate, as any addict does, one day at a time or even minute by minute. At first, it was easy because that final scene, which climaxed in the police-drama-crescendo, fortified me with lots of bravado. But as the memory of that incident eventually faded, there were times when I was tempted to give in to my cravings to see Richard again. The good news is that I didn't. I realize now that those times didn't *have* to be so daunting, but I can also see why they were: because I was resisting what happened. I wanted it to be different. I wanted Richard to be my *ideal* of him rather than the person he actually was. My strong preferences and mental constructs caused my agony— nothing else.

In finally letting go of him and going through the stages of grief, I noticed that the first four stages—anger, denial, bargaining, and depression — are all about resisting what is. When you get to the last stage of acceptance, you finally have relief because you're no longer pushing against what happened anymore. So why not just jump to acceptance and skip all of the other steps? Good question. Some would say that you have to honor your feelings and the process, but if there's a way to feel better sooner, why not accelerate it? What if every time I notice my resistance, I make a bold attempt to start the willful practice of surrendering my preferences of what I *wish* was happening to accepting what *is*? The bee has stung. I can be upset and go through all sorts of gyrations, or I can replace the meaningless noise while taking some deep breaths, applying first aid measures, and noticing how the change in my focus has quieted things down. (Remember: the cortisol released by your limbic system, which causes you to react to a perceived threat, can be calmed by deep breathing. That breathing activates the von Economo neurons in the ACC.)

Moving Mountains

> *I tell you the truth. If you have faith as small as a mustard seed and you say to this mountain, "Move from here to there," it will move. Nothing will be impossible for you.*
>
> *—Matthew 17:20*

If you take into consideration everything we've been discussing about human evolution, including various examples of why we may default to operating at primal levels (i.e. resistance), you can easily see why we can behave unconsciously. So, at the risk of sounding cheesy, you kind of have to become a warrior for light and love in order to tackle the dark forces of your lower nature. Of course, taking that warrior path means you have to fortify yourself with perseverance, since those dark forces are deeply embedded in each of us. As can happen with any warrior who sets out on a challenging mission, you're likely to experience some defeats. Those can make you stronger if you let them—something I know by heart.

Over time, with patience, love, trust, and determination, you will eventually attain victory over those dark forces. When you do, you'll live primarily in peace, harmony, and freedom. Finally liberated from some of the impulses of your limbic system (like dopamine-drive desire), you'll look back on who or what it was that motivated you to drop into your heart and feel tremendous gratitude for that person, event, or both. You'll then realize that every single relationship you've had in your life—however brief, lengthy, challenging, or profound—is *significant*. Each one has given you an opportunity to become that warrior for light and love, regardless of how the person showed up in your orbit. Therefore, you'll hold all in the highest regard for their service to you. Through this honoring, you'll transcend your struggle altogether—no more resistance—and experience only total acceptance of everything and everyone.

The perseverance required to cultivate your warrior spirit will strengthen your self-regulation circuits, which will support you in overriding challenges, including any addictive tendencies—either behavioral like mine, or otherwise. When you decide to let Life be in charge, you'll systematically let go of insoluble problems one by one. The dives and dramas just won't captivate you anymore. And as you actually do let go, unhinging yourself from your mental gridlock, you'll create space for Divine love to resolve any lingering longing.

This love lives both in you and around you. It's the mighty power that sleeps in your substance (per Thibon), taking form now as the brilliant part of your being coming into focus. It's that undeniable force that you know you can channel to move mountains. It's the life urge, which will keep directing you to the soul of your self-belonging, where insoluble problems no longer have any potency.

Putting to Rest the Unrest — Flipping the Switch

It is my personal belief that the state of deep human unrest showing up in a variety of ways — anything from mental illness, to addictions, to deep-seated positions on this or that — has its roots in the tendency of humanity to rely on the primal. We do this instead of flipping the switch to turn on the upgrade.

You're like a house that has been completely remodeled and pre-wired with state-of-the-art equipment. You just need a little instruction from your designer to explain how to operate the new stuff. That Divine architect is standing by to show you how to turn the lights on. All you have to do is pay attention and remember where that switch is — even if you need lots of guidance, and you may, sometimes — over and over, until you're comfortable navigating the new territory.

It isn't easy living in these body-suits here on planet Earth, where there are plenty of distractions to drive us toward relief. When we're hungry, we indulge our appetite, but once satisfied by a meal, it won't be long until that sense of gratification fades. Then, we're off looking for the next banquet — tempted to blame the steak dinner or perhaps the Prince/Princess (in my case, Richard) for not being the lasting solution for our insatiable longing. We can become addicted to the person or thing we perceive as the source of our delight unless we wake up to the pain/pleasure cycle that snared us and kept us stuck.

According to researcher, philosopher, and visionary Richard Rudd, "It is because of this basic pattern of disappointment (attachment/addiction) and blame that the human spirit is unable to find lasting peace." Luckily for us, there have been others before us who have thrown out many a lifeline or shown us a wormhole—Jesus, Buddha, Eckhart, Jung, and Rumi, as well as Christian mystics, Hildegard of Bingen, and Julian of Norwich, to name a few. They have demonstrated that we absolutely *can* upgrade into the Divine blueprint and actualize the most optimal versions of ourselves.

Over the course of the past several months, I've noticed some pretty interesting changes in myself. While nothing much is different in my external world, aside from the obvious signs of aging, my inner landscape feels significantly altered from what I was experiencing just a couple of years ago. That was before I turned to look at and listen to God instead of the imposters I had repeatedly positioned in God's place. It continues to be empowering to take back all arrows of accusation and own my part in any misery I experienced—particularly as I reinforce the practice with love and compassion for both myself and those I'd previously blamed for my pain.

Things started to shift when I released a flood of repressed emotions through sitting in the stew of my pain, praying, contemplating, journaling, hiking, meditating, doing yoga, and seeking spiritual direction from wise teachers. After a while, I began to realize I'd consistently been waking up each morning in a good mood for no particular reason I could identify. It certainly wasn't because I was having that all powerful instant high I used to crave—the one I'd get when the phone would finally ring with Richard on the other end. Instead, I was just happy to be alive, happy I was awake, and happy to make a cup of coffee for one.

There have been predictable dips when my mind ruminates on this or that—all the old familiar stuff. Nonetheless, as I've persevered with my practices, slowly, steadily, I've watched the patterns of the past diminish as some higher and wider interest has appeared on my horizon—beyond my little local self and all of her fears, needs, desires, and attachments.

While in the process, as predicted by Mathew Fox's fourfold path of spiritual evolution—via positiva, via negativa, via creativa, via transformativa—my good moods have been consistently accompanied by periods of expanding creativity. *Hallelujah! This stuff is working*—neuroplasticity, epigenetics, strengthened ACC (flooded with more and more von Economo neurons), increased self-regulation circuits, and all. In addition, I suspect that my dopamine levels are evening out, accompanied by an appropriate supply of serotonin (a neurotransmitter that regulates mood, appetite, and sleep).

As for the transformativa, the last stage of Matthew Fox's fourfold path, I have definitely experienced some brief periods of transformation, though I'm surely not enlightened. I *definitely* still get triggered and often forget what to do when that happens, but I just keep sharpening the tools that mitigate my reactions. Besides, if we aren't careful, can't the pursuit of enlightenment be another setup to long for fulfillment in something unattainable—not unlike the ideal of romance, the fairy tale, and true love's kiss by Prince Charming? Could transformation (transformativa/transcendence) or freedom from suffering (which, by the way, doesn't necessarily mean freedom from pain) be nothing more than knocking down the walls of illusion that cause us to believe there's something out there like enlightenment to set us free?

As we've repeatedly discussed, getting free can only happen when we dive into what Thibon called that narrow place within. Slowly, steadily, when we keep on shoveling, staying present, and paying attention to what we find in that narrow place, gratitude just becomes a way of life. And can't the very act of feeling grateful support you in surrendering your ego's preferences, while deferring to Divine judgment?

Self-belonging — A Final Test

Dear Reader, all of my theories about self-regulation, dopamine-driven desire, thriving alone, and outgrowing insoluble problems came to a final test when I was finishing this manuscript. While finessing my conclusions about life, romance, and the path ahead, someone from my very distant past showed up — literally on my doorstep. Alex was a man to whom I was deeply devoted in my early twenties several decades ago. He was probably my first real love, although my understanding of real love is very different now than it was back then. He lives on the other side of the continent and just happened to be in the area about the time his divorce was finalized. He asked if he could come for a visit.

It had been three years since I'd closed the Richard chapter. Despite some anticipatory anxiety, I was willing to open my heart and see what might happen. It felt like a brave move.

I suspect my subconscious mind had positioned this man in the soulmate category over the course of the many years we'd lived completely apart. He was married and living on a different continent, and I was a single social worker researching the riddles of human consciousness. I'd always wondered if it had been a mistake to leave him behind so long ago when he was focused on school and career rather than our future together. When it seemed obvious to me that he wasn't interested in marrying me and settling down, I left the relationship without telling him my true feelings of wanting marriage and kids. I was fragile back then and afraid of being shattered if I had the truth spelled out for me that he didn't want the same things. So rather than confront my fear about what he might say, I walked. Perhaps his visit would provide another opportunity for us to reconnect. If I'd tried to design a more perfect final exam for myself in this course of self-belonging — just about the time I was ready to turn this material over to you—I couldn't have done better.

As soon as Alex entered the scene, I certainly felt that old, familiar desire crackling and popping—destined to take over if I couldn't get a grip. Could I call up those self-regulation circuits I'd been cultivating? Thankfully, for the most part, I was able to observe the scene as it unfolded in front of me rather than get all swept up in it. As much as my romantic side was all-a-twitter about our rendezvous, I focused instead on the true gift that his first visit reaffirmed for me: as I come into Divine alignment where that life urge has the strongest voice, the longing dissolves inch by inch and cell by cell.

It was obvious from the beginning of this most recent encounter that Alex and I had grown philosophically apart over the many years since we'd seen each other. Nonetheless, he seemed to have maintained his solid character and values over the years, is handsome, bright, and enjoys some of the same activities I do. Also, we'd been in love for a long time when we were young, and the chemistry between us still seemed to be alive. I did my best to surrender to this new development in my love life while deferring to the Indwelling God: could I dig down into that narrow space where no sound but a hymn to the heavens could be heard? Regardless of what was going to happen (or not happen) with Alex, I would bathe myself in unconditional love. Fortunately, I had the faith to believe that love would sustain me, and isn't that, dear readers, what self-belonging is all about?

Amazing Grace

In *The Road Less Traveled,* Scott Peck describes acts of Grace as serendipitous events when you receive valuable things not asked for. One such act of Grace occurred just prior to Alex's arrival. I'd received some mementos from an acquaintance that brought me back to that dream I had twenty years ago (described in Chapter Five)—

the inspiration for my first book. When I awoke the morning of the dream, I felt like it was real and being awake was the illusion. From that moment on, I knew on every level that the powerful feeling of unconditional love available in that dream (I still have no vocabulary to describe it) was meant to represent our most natural human state. I knew, too, that I'd devote the rest of my life to expanding into that state and would write about my experiences and findings in order to support others in doing the same.

As I sat with Alex gazing upon the dream-reminder gifts I'd been sent, I felt the same feelings of unconditional love I'd had in that dream. It was because of those feelings that I was almost effortlessly able to surrender the outcome of our rekindled romance. I realized that if I didn't let go on every level, I would end up losing myself again in an effort to fit into his world, while trying to convince him to mold himself to meet mine. Or I'd cut off from him completely to avoid any possible pain.

Instead of reverting back into the fairy tale ideal in my relationship with Alex, I have wanted to keep replicating my dream's feelings of unconditional love. I have wanted to focus on loving him exactly as he is without a need for him to change, just as I want to love myself through and through. This has been my way of using the relationship as a spiritual practice and allowing whatever comes up between us to be an opportunity for negotiating a favorable connection regardless of our differences (and perhaps even because of them). If Alex and I discover that the relationship isn't sustainable, I've stayed committed to managing whatever disappointment might arise as another way to access that narrow space. In short, I'm determined to grow in Alex's presence or in his absence, repeatedly digging in to let go of outcomes. When I can remember to do so, it's an *enormous* relief to sit in the lap of the Divine while letting Her guide things. Rather than assuming I know what's best, I can let go of my ego's preferences, open the space for the Divine to shine Her light on my next moves, and release the fairy tale—trusting, in fact *knowing,* that the right path will be revealed.

I absolutely believe that when we're centered in Divine love, the right relationships will continue to flourish in our lives, while the ones that aren't in alignment with our soul's destiny and purpose will simply fall away. True love *will* continue to reveal itself as we dive more and more deeply into love itself at the core of our essence. We *don't* have to go looking for it. It will just appear again and again in the faces of our friends, lovers, children, and grandchildren. In continuing to strengthen the Inner Beloved, we will move closer and closer to God-consciousness and continuously discover that we're capable of the utterly miraculous.

As your personal research project, I see this most recent connection with Alex, occurring simultaneously with the completion of this material, as an extraordinary blessing. I can watch my patterns emerge and desist one more time in the fields of my own consciousness and share the experience with you in the final phase of this conversation we're having.

And when I find myself upset and wanting either to shoot off the arrow or dissolve into a state of tearful wallowing about how unfair it all is, I know that's the time to be *alert and aware.* Then, I can acknowledge how I've been hooked.

This is exactly how you can avoid reacting by blaming someone or something else for your suffering or by stuffing your feelings and playing the victim in your own drama. What you're learning is that it isn't about what happens to you in life but what happens *through* you and how you handle it all. That's what will determine the pace of your conscious evolution. How will you respond to the circumstances in front of you? Will you feel victimized when things don't go your way, or will you be able to take full responsibility for your part? Can you use whatever is going on to take you beyond your little, local self?

In letting go of your temptation to cling to ideas of what you like or don't like about something or someone, your reactions will softly melt into responses. Maybe you'll decide to silence your opinion altogether, creating a space to discover the most important part of any scenario that's triggering you. What's being asked of you in this situation? What would happen if you didn't resist it? Following the guidance from that narrow place within might just take you to a very different and distinctly better destination than where your original preferences would have guided you.

As you continue to step back in the moment from whatever is disturbing your peace of mind—without a need to fix or change it—you build emotional resilience. You recruit God consciousness, which is the only way to truly resolve pain. When you're willing to sit in your discomfort and let it cook you a bit, you'll find without exception, you'll always simmer down. When you do, you create an opening to dive down deep, where the Divine can work Her magic. Indulging in distractions to ease your distress will only increase your pain by pinching off the pathways for God to find a way into your heart. Every addictive tendency is an unwillingness to face or cover up your pain—no exceptions.

> *There, where clinging to things ends, is where God begins to be. If a cask is to contain wine, you must first pour out the water. The cask must be bare and empty. Therefore, if you wish to receive divine joy and God, first pour out your clinging to things. Everything that is to receive must be and ought to be empty. It is a delusion to think that we can obtain more of God by contemplation or by pious devotions or by religious retreats than by being at the fireplace or by working*

in the stable. For the person who has learned letting
go and letting be no creature can any longer hinder.
Rather, each creature points you toward God and
toward new birth and toward seeing the world as God
sees it: Transparently! Thus all things become nothing
but God. And we learn to know with God's knowledge
and to live with God's love.

—Meister Eckhart

Can you influence your own destiny by tapping into the full potential dialed into your DNA? Do you have a choice in how your reality is constructed? If so, how do you create your own reality? Richard Rudd posits that you actually can and will experience an alchemical transformation as you raise your consciousness through love. As he writes in *The Gene Keys:*

Delicate chemical matrices actually begin to take
place in your physiology, which causes your ... inner
essence to be refined and distilled in the endocrine
system.... The easiest and quickest way to change your
life for the better is to give your love unconditionally
in as many areas of your life as you dare. If you
take on this adventure, you will actually affect the
minute workings of your DNA. You will stimulate new
chemical messages to pass from gene to gene and you
will enter a whole new world of adventure.... [For]
written into the human DNA is a great evolutionary
(master) plan.... Pure unconditional love can break all
the laws of the cosmos.

As it turns out, according to Rudd (with whom I heartily agree), love—the cosmic version—is the magic catalyzer that speeds up our evolutionary plan.

Sam Keen writes in his classic book, *To Love and Be Loved*, a favorite quote shared earlier: "In the depths of our being, in body, mind, and spirit, we know intuitively that we are created to love and be loved, and that fulfilling this imperative, responding to this vocation, is the central meaning to our life." In that spirit, dear reader, I want to continue loving with all of the gusto I can muster.

> *There is no difficulty that enough love will not conquer: no disease that love will not heal: no door that enough love will not open…. It makes no difference how deep set the trouble: how hopeless the outlook: how muddled the tangle: how great the mistake. A sufficient realization of love will dissolve it all. If only you could love enough you would be the happiest and most powerful being in the world.*
>
> *—Emmet Fox*

Of course, loving *yourself* enough is your launch pad to self-belonging. Thank you for helping me remember. As I've written these words for you, they have first been written for me.

Addendum

My dear Readers,

Remarkably, it has been almost four years since I started writing the epilogue you may have just finished reading—in the middle of which Alex re-emerged after about a half-century hiatus. I dotted the last "i" and crossed the last "t" of that epilogue nearly two years ago— literally a few hours before I set out for the East Coast to help Alex celebrate his birthday.

Even though we hadn't explicitly discussed commitment over our two years together, there were many indicators that having a long-term partnership was the direction in which we were headed. Yet, consistent with his communication style during our first romance, Alex made no clear pledges or promises. So, fortified by an ever-strengthening self-belonging spirit, as well as a seemingly more loving and open Alex this time around, I asked his thoughts on going forward a few days after my arrival. You'll recall that years ago I made my exit without asking him that question— since he never volunteered the information (not so different from this time). I was afraid of what the truth might have been back then. Remarkably, nearly fifty years later, I've found my ongoing commitment to self-belong has paid off. This time, I *wanted* to know the truth—no matter what.

"I'm not ready to commit. I just don't know if this is it," Alex flatly announced after three martinis (truth serum?), seemingly dissociating from any level of sensitivity or respect. When my jaw dropped to my knees following that cold, flat, insult, he quickly added the following addendum: "I mean forever and ever," perhaps hoping the awkwardly tacked on after-thought was going to somehow soften the preceding message?

ADDENDUM

"Thank you for your honesty," I said, in as measured and calm a tone as I could conjure. I then turned on my heels and ascended the very long three flights of stairs to the guest quarters in his perfectly appointed town-home. Once safely behind the latched door, feeling a bit like Rapunzel, I pondered my escape route: *Maybe I can recruit some Rapunzel chutzpa, slap on some hair extensions to serve as rope, and discreetly make my exit through the window without Alex being any the wiser?*

Previous to my ascent to Rapunzel's tower, I did muster up some magic from the Internal Divine, who whispered, "Don't let yourself lose me." By remembering She was there to walk me silently out of the night, I was reminded to take a few breaths before I was tempted to tack on a cynical zinger to the statement I'd managed to eke out ("Thank you for your honesty.") As a result, my old pattern of playing victim and projecting blame dissolved. Miraculously, in replacing that pattern, I instantly had compassion for both of us. What had happened was just a moment of that truth I'd willingly solicited (likely strengthened by his belt full of booze). That was all. Even though my ego wanted to include something like, *You arrogant prick,* fortunately, I was able to put a lid on that one after taking some *very* deep breaths. Thank you, Economo neurons.

Fortified with grit and gumption up in Rapunzel's tower, I called the friendly skies of United and got the next available flight out of Dodge, deciding to make a civilized exit (instead of jumping out the window) and face Alex courageously the next day. "You are the one," Alex declared, in his farewell hug at the airport. I made my way to the terminal door without responding. When I turned to wave goodbye, I mouthed, *I love you,* flashing on Emmet Fox's words: "If only you could love enough, you would be the happiest and most powerful being in the world." Alex nodded, acknowledging my gesture, not realizing, I'm almost certain, that it would be the last time I would ever utter those words to him. I'd loved him for fifty years. I was finally complete.

As I turned to enter the terminal, I thought, Yes. I *am* the one—the one settling back into my own seat of belonging, reflecting on words I'd written earlier: *I could never again allow someone to crush all manner of logic in me*—even Alex, a man I'd probably loved for the majority of my life. As much as I didn't want to believe it, he was just not a "forever and ever" kinda guy. Of course, you and I know there is no such thing as forever and ever. Nonetheless, that declaration,"…just not forever and ever," was, to me, a perfect representation of what I'd known him always to be—the sort of man that wanted to keep his options open—just in case he might decide to shop around for something "better." ("I just don't know if this is it.") It's how he operated a few decades ago, and it's how he operates now. Finally recognizing this fact was an *enormous* blessing. Alex and I were not a fit—we had different truths and models of the world. Remarkably, I am *completely* okay with that, as I nestle back in to my self-belonging skin. In fact, extraordinarily so, after realizing the incredible serendipity of being able to complete this manuscript with the astonishing reminder of what *true* self-belonging really means. I have tremendous gratitude for Alex, for there is likely no one else on the planet who could have driven the self-belonging point home to me more vividly than he. At last, my heart, logic, and soul prevail—*hallelujah*!

Rilke's words have *enormous* value, "Just keep going. No feeling is final. Don't let yourself lose me.… Give me your hand." And so, I extend that hand to the Divine, yet another time to lead, guide, direct, and protect me—I can't wait to see where She takes me. Thank you with *all of my heart* for joining me on this journey, still in progress—please stay tuned for the handbook to accompany this material, now well underway, and coming soon!

ADDENDUM

With my love I am faithfully yours,
  Luann Robinson Hull

Acknowledgments

When a miracle unfolds, you can look back and see the Divine hand that superbly wove together the tapestry of people, places, events, and circumstances to create the phenomenon. This book, to me, represents such a miracle. It began with my conversation on Christmas Eve, 2011, with the extraordinary man who planted the seed for self-belonging. Immediately after hearing his touching story of being abandoned by his family at the age of seven and subsequent decision to belong to himself, I sat down at my computer and downloaded the poem that appears at the beginning of Chapter One— launching the material you now hold in your hands.

After many beginning drafts—and thanks to my dear chum and colleague, Rita Marsh, for connecting us—I began handing off the material to my now cherished friend and editor, Karen Connington, whose exquisite eye for detail, together with her extraordinary wisdom and heart, patiently helped guide and refine this book. Without her, this project wouldn't have been possible. My thanks to Teri Rider of Top Reads Publishing for her contributions in bringing this book into form, and to Melanie Voltaw for her thoughts on rearranging our text. Peggy Burke's copy editing wizardry added the final polish to this work, for which I am so grateful.

Over the course of the last few months, Brandi Flittner, social media and marketing expert, has joined our *Self Belonging* team, and is responsible for assembling the manuscript for final print, combining her graphic and cover design mastery to create the finished product. Having Brandi in our midst is an endless blessing.

My dear friend and gifted colleague, Jean Watson, Dean Emerita of the University of Colorado Denver, College of Nursing, and founder of the Watson Caring Science Institute, was the first to step forward in endorsing this book. I deeply cherish her words of support, as well as the others who have sanctioned my work.

This material has its foundation in the wisdom of a multitude of spiritual leaders and scientific wizards whose insights are entwined throughout. I'm certain you will want to ponder each one, as you consider how you, too, may be called to participate (or continue participating) in upgrading our human potential.

I am infinitely grateful to my dear friends, family, and spiritual directors, who have stalwartly stood by my side through all of my trials and victories as I have brought this material into form. How dearly I have been blessed to have each one of them in my life.

Also, I offer my thanks to all of the boys and men, with whom I have been involved at various times in my life, including those mentioned in this material. I have been repeatedly guided by their tutelage to understand that the only way to experience a true and lasting partner is to first decide to belong to and partner with myself.

Finally, I am most grateful of all for my late parents Catherine and Lewis; my loving and loyal brother Steve; my dear sister-in-law, Patty; my late sister-in-law, Vicki; my amazing sons, Nes and Stephen; my lovely daughter-in-law, Laura; my precious Grandchildren, Vivien and Theo; and my former husband, Nestor, who gifted me with our two treasured sons.

In service to Consciousness, I am faithfully yours,

Luann Robinson Hull

Bibliography

A Course in Miracles. Foundation for Inner Peace, 1992.

Alexander, Eben. *Proof of Heaven: A Neurosurgeon's Journey into the Afterlife*. Simon & Schuster, 2012.

Allan, D.S., and J.B. Delair. *Cataclysm!: Compelling Evidence of a Cosmic Catastrophe in 9500 B.C.* Bear & Company, 1997.

Avatar. Directed by James Cameron, 20th Century Fox, 2009.

Backman, Linda. *Bringing Your Soul to Light: Healing Through Past Lives and the Time Between*. Llewellyn Publications, 2009

Barnard, Anne. "Joining the Jihadists." New York Times Book Review, 2019, November 10, p. 39.

The Bhagavad Gita. Translated by Gavin Flood and Charles Martin, W.W. Norton Company, 2012.

The Bible. King James Version, Frank J. Thompson Publishing, 1929.

Bishop, Ross. *Healing the Shadow*. Blue Lotus Press, 2012.

Bolen, Jean Shinoda. *Goddesses in Older Women*. HarperCollins, 2001.

Brown, Brené. *The Power of Vulnerability*. Ted Talks, March 4, 2014.

Campbell, Joseph. *Hero's Journey: Joseph Campbell on His Life and Work*. New World Library, 2014

—. *Pathways to Bliss: Mythology and Personal Transformation*. New World Library, 2004.

Chodron, Pema. *Taking the Leap: Freeing Ourselves from Old Habits and Fears*. Shambala, 2009.

Chopra, Deepak. *Ageless Body, Timeless Mind: The Quantum Alternative to Growing Old*. Harmony Books, 1994.

Clow, Barbara Hand. *Awakening the Planetary Mind: Beyond the Trauma of the Past to a New Era of Creativity*. Bear & Company, 2011.

Dacher, Elliott S. *Aware, Awake, Alive: A Contemporary Guide to the Ancient Science of Integral Health and Human Flourishing.* Paragon House, 2011.

Davies, James B., and Anthony F. Shorrocks. "Comparing Global Inequality of Income and Wealth." *The United Nations University World Institute for Development Economics Research*, WIDER Working Paper 160/2018, www.doi.org/10.35188/UNU-WIDER/2018/602-9.

Declaration of Independence, Philadelphia, Pennsylvania, 1776.

Declaration of Sentiments, Women's Rights Convention, 1848.

Dowling, Colette. *The Cinderella Complex: Women's Hidden Fear of Independence.* Pocket Books, 1990.

Eliot, Thomas Stearns. *The Four Quartets.* Houghton Mifflin Harcourt, 1950.

Emancipation Proclamation, U.S. Constitution. Amendment XIII.

Fat Guys in the Woods. Directed by Gary Johnson and Carl Merenda, The Weather Channel, 2014.

Fonda, Jane. National Women's Leadership Conference, 2003, Washington D.C.

Fox, Matthew. *The Original Blessing.* Bear & Company, 1983.

— . *Meditations with Meister Eckhart.* Bear & Company, 1983.

Fox, Matthew, and Rupert Sheldrake. *Natural Grace: Dialogues on Science and Spirituality.* Image, 1997.

Friday, Nancy. *My Mother, Myself: The Daughter's Search for Identity.* Delta, 1997.

Gabriel, Peter. "In Your Eyes." *So*, Geffen, 1986.

Gay, Peter. *Freud: A Life for Our Time.* W.W. Norton & Company, 1988.

Gibran, Kahlil. *The Prophet.* Alfred A. Knopf, 1923.

Gilligan, Carol. *In a Different Voice: Psychological Theory and Women's Development.* Harvard University Press, 1982.

Goleman, Daniel and Richard J. Davidson. *The Science of Medi-*

201

tation: How to Change Your Brain, Mind and Body. Penguin Live, 2018.

Hartmann, Thom. *Unequal Protection: The Rise of Corporate Dominance and the Theft of Human Rights.* Rodale Books, 2004.

—. *The Last Hours of Ancient Sunlight. Waking Up To Personal and Global Transformation.* Three Rivers Press, 1998, 1999.

Hawkins, David R. *Transcending the Levels of Consciousness: The Stairway to Enlightenment.* Veritas Publishing, 2006.

Hubbard, Barbara Marx. *Conscious Evolution: Awakening the Power of Our Social Potential.* New World Library, 1998.

James, EL. *Fifty Shades of Grey.* Vintage Books, 2011

Janis, Irving L. *Groupthink: Psychological Studies of Policy Decisions and Fiascoes.* Cengage Learning, 1982.

Joplin, Janis. "Me and Bobby McGee." *Pearl,* Columbia Records, 1971.

Jung, C.G. C.G. *Jung: Psychological Reflections. A New Anthology of His Writings, 1905-1961.* Edited and translated by Jolande Jacobi, translated by R.F.C. Hull, Princeton University Press, 1973.

Keen, Sam. *To Love and Be Loved.* Bantam, 1999.

Kidd, Sue Monk. *The Invention of Wings.* Viking Press, 2014.

"Lance's Fender Bender." *Aspen Times,* February 6, 2015.

LeDoux, Joseph. *The Emotional Brain.* Simon & Schuster, 1998.

Legrand, Michel, Jacques Demy and Norman Gimbel. "I Will Wait for You." *The Umbrellas of Cherbourg,* 1964.

Lipton, Bruce H. *Spontaneous Evolution (And a Way to Get There from Here).* Hay House, 2009.

Maltz, Maxwell. *Psycho-Cybernetics: A New Way to Get More Out of Life.* Tarcher Perigee, 2015.

Maté, Gabor. *In the Realm of Hungry Ghosts: Close Encounters with Addiction.* Knopf Canada, 2008.

BIBLIOGRAPHY

McDonald, Michael. "Sweet Freedom." *No Lookin' Back*, Warner Brothers, 1986.

McLaren, Karla. *The Language of Emotion: What Your Feelings Are Trying to Tell You*. Sounds True, 2010.

Minority Report. Directed by Steven Spielberg, 20th Century Fox, 2002.

Newberg, Andrew, and Mark Robert Waldman. *How God Changes the Brain: Breakthrough Findings from a Leading Neuroscientist*. Ballantine Books, 2009.

Newton, Michael. *Journey of Souls: Case Studies of Life Between Lives*. Llewellyn Publications, 2002.

Norwood, Robin. *Women Who Love Too Much: When You Keep Wishing and Hoping He'll Change*. Pocket Books, 1990.

Peck, Scott M. *The Road Less Traveled: A New Psychology of Love, Traditional Values and Spiritual Growth*. Simon & Schuster, 1978.

Pinchbeck, Daniel. *2012 The Return of Quetzalcoatl*. Tarcher/Penguin, 2007.

Rilke, Rainer Maria. *Rilke's Book of Hours: Love Poems to God*. Translated by Anita Barrows and Joanna Macy, Riverhead Books, 1997.

Rubin, Alissa J. and Aurelien Breeden. "Female French Jihadists Signal Shift in ISIS Roles." *New York Times*, 2016, October 2, Section A, p.6.

Rudd, Richard. *The Gene Keys: Unlocking the Higher Purpose Hidden in Your DNA*. Watkins Publishing, 2013.

Rumi, Jalal ad-Din Muhammad. *The Big Red Book*. Translated by Coleman Barks, HarperCollins, 2010.

—. *The Essential Rumi,* translated by Coleman Barks. HarperOne, 2004.

Simon, Carly and Michael McDonald. "You Belong to Me." *Boys in the Trees*, Elektra, 1978.

Sin by Silence. Directed by Olivia Klaus, Women Make Movies, 2009.

Singer, Michael. *The Untethered Soul: The Journey Beyond Yourself*. New Harbinger Publications, 2007.

Stern, Jess. *The Search for a Soul: Taylor Caldwell's Psychic Lives*. Doubleday & Company, 1973.

Steve Jobs. Directed by Danny Boyle, Universal Pictures, 2015.

Sting. "If I Ever Lose My Faith in You." *Ten Summoner's Tales,* A&M, 1993.

—. "Mad About You." *Ten Summoner's Tales,* A&M, 1993.

Stryker, Rod. *The Four Desires*. Penguin/Random House, 2011.

Tendulkar, D.G. *MAHATMA Life of Mohandas Karamchand Gandhi Volume 2*. The Publications Division Ministry of Information and Broadcasting Government of India, 1951.

"The Frozen Planet." *Planet Earth*, BBC Natural History Unit and Discovery Channel, Winter, 2011.

U.S. Constitution. Amendment XIX.

Van Meter, Jonathan. "Adele: One and Only." *Vogue,* Feb 13, 2012.

Viorst, Judith. *Necessary Losses: The Loves Illusions Dependencies and Impossible Expectations That All of us Have*. Simon & Schuster, 1998.

Vitale, Joe, and Ihaleakala Hew Len. *Zero Limits: The Secret Hawaiian System for Wealth, Health, Peace, and More*. Wiley and Sons, 2007.

Weiss, Brian L. *Many Lives Many Masters: The True Story of a Prominent Psychiatrist, His Young Patient, and the Past Life Therapy That Changed Both Their Lives*. Touchstone, 1988.

Whyte, David. "Self Portrait." *Fire in the Earth,* Many Rivers Press, 1992.

—. "Sweet Darkness." *River Flow: New & Selected Poems 1984-2007,* Many Rivers Press, 2007.

Wilcock, David. *The Source Field Investigations: The Hidden Science and Lost Civilizations Behind the 2012 Prophecies*. Dutton, 2011.

—. *The Synchronicity Key: The Hidden Intelligence Guiding the Universe and You*. Dutton, 2013.

Winwood, Steve. "Bring Me A Higher Love." *Back in the High Life,*

Island Records, 1986.

ONLINE REFERENCES

Fox, Matthew. "The Courageous Mystic Course." *The Shift Network*, 2 July – 9 August 2020, www. theshiftnetwork.com/course/Coura-geousMystic. Accessed 2 July 2020.

Hartoonian Almas, Linda. "Intermittent reinforcement: conditioning helps explain why we stay with abusive individuals." *Lovefraud. com.*, 2013 27 June, www.lovefraud.com/intermittent-reinforce-ment-conditioning-helps-explain-stay-abusive-individuals. Accessed 8 July 2017.

Hassett-Walker, Connie. "What the Salem witches can teach us about how we treat women today." *The Washington Post*, 2018, June 10, *www.washingtonpost.com/news/made-by-history/wp/2018/06/10/what-the-salem-witches-can-teach-us-about-how-we-treat-women-today*. Accessed 23 July 2019.

Huecker, Martin R., and William Smock. "Domestic Violence." *University of Louisville*, updated 2020 15 October, www.ncbi.nlm.nih.gov/books/NBK499891/. Accessed 10 November 2020.

Lally, Phillippa, Cornelia H. M. van Jaarsveld, Henry W. W. Potts, and Jane Wardle. "How Are Habits Formed: Modeling Habit Formation in the Real World." *European Journal of Social Psychology,* vol. 39, 2009, www.doi.org/10.1002/ejsp.674. Accessed 22 September 2015.

Livingston, Gretchen. "The Changing Profile of Unmarried Parents." *Pew Research Center,* 2018 25 April, www.pewsocialtrends.org/2018/04/25/the-changing-profile-of-unmarried-parents/. Accessed 26 November 2020.

McLeod, Saul. "Maslow's Hierarchy of Needs." SimplyPsychology, updated 2020 29 December, www.simplypsychology.org/maslow.html. Accessed 4 January, 2020.

Percz-Chisti, Ana. *www.sufiuniversalfraternalinstitute.live*. Accessed 14 September 2017.

Shantay, Eaden. *www.truenaturehealingarts.com/about*. Accessed 7

May 2018.

"The State of the Gender Pay Gap, 2020." *Payscale.com*, www.pay-scale.com/data/gender-pay-gap. Accessed 22 November 2020.

Wheatley, Margaret. *www. margaretwheatley.com*. Accessed 17 January 2018.

Thank you for reading!

Dear Reader,

I hope you enjoyed *Self Belonging: Embrace the Wisdom of Soul and Science to Live Your Best Life*.

As an author, I appreciate getting feedback. I would enjoy hearing your thoughts and your own stories of your experiences after you read my book. You can write me at the addresses below.

Like all authors, I rely on online reviews to encourage future sales. You, the reader, have the power to influence other readers to share your journey with a book you've read. In fact, most readers pick their next book because of a review or on the advice of a friend. So, your opinion is invaluable. Would you take a few moments now to share your assessment of my book on Amazon, Goodreads or any other book review website you prefer? Your opinion will help the book marketplace become more transparent and useful to all.

Thank you so much for reading *Self Belonging,* and if you are so inclined, please visit the links below to learn more about how you, too, can live your best life.

Luann Robinson Hull
luannjlt@aol.com
luannrobinsonhull.com
Instagram: LuannRHull
facebook: @LuannRobinsonHull

About the Author

Luann Robinson Hull is a trailblazing leader in the field of human development. With a Masters in Clinical Social Work, and a Doctorate in Ministry, she brings a powerfully diverse background to the world of personal growth and well-being. Her twenty-five-year career, which includes researching both neuroscience and spiritual practices that help to transcend maladaptive patterns of behavior, allows her to be a reliable and definitive expert on how to unravel the ravages of the mind.

Luann is a motivational speaker and professional group facilitator. She resides in the mountains of Colorado where she hikes year-round, often in a state of curiosity inspired by Thoreau's idea that we "spend one day as deliberately as Nature, and not be thrown off the track by every nutshell and mosquito's wing that falls on the rails."

Made in the USA
Las Vegas, NV
13 April 2024

88561055R00121